ISLANDS
AND
LIFELINES

John Plummer.

JOHN PLUMMER

ISLANDS
AND
LIFELINES

Journeys with friends from across a lifetime to
the dramatic edges of Britain and Ireland

www.islandsandlifelines.co.uk

Matador
9 De Montfort Mews
Leicester LE1 7FW, UK
Tel: (+44) 116 255 9311 / 9312
Email: books@troubador.co.uk
Web: www.troubador.co.uk/matador

A contribution will be made from the sales of this book to the Neuropathy Trust
which promotes awareness of Peripheral Neuropathy

ISBN 978 1906510 930

A Cataloguing-in-Publication (CIP) catalogue record for this book
is available from the British Library.

Mixed Sources
Product group from well-managed
forests and other controlled sources
www.fsc.org Cert no. TT-COC-2082
© 1996 Forest Stewardship Council

Typeset in 11pt Bembo by Troubador Publishing Ltd, Leicester, UK
Printed in the UK by The Cromwell Press Ltd, Trowbridge, Wilts, UK

Matador is an imprint of Troubador Publishing Ltd

This book is dedicated to my fellow travellers

CONTENTS

ACKNOWLEDGEMENTS

This book would never have appeared without the help and encouragement of a lot of people, some of whom deserve specific mention. First I must thank my ten fellow travellers for their enthusiasm in all sorts of winds and weather and for their patience as I pursued the many loose strands of my venture. My reader-in-chief, Richard Plummer, has offered astute and frank comment in a skilful manner. My journey as a new writer was guided wisely by David Selzer and Julia McCutchen, who also led me into the serpentine ways of publishing. Of the writers I approached just two responded – Mark Wallington and Sarah Poyntz, both of whom were very positive. Much appreciated. My photography improved with tuition from No-Limits (Malpas), Nick Jenkins and Cathy Taylor. Katie Dunn provided skilled proof-reading. Finally the help of Terry Compton and colleagues at Matador was invaluable.

Photographs in colour and further information about the project and the book can be found at

www.islandsandlifelines.co.uk

FOREWORD

THIS IS A PERSONAL JOURNEY to inspirational places with important friends from across my life. This venture took place between 2005 and 2007. The planning was shared but most of the research is my own, so responsibility for any errors or offence caused here is mine. We travelled happily, purposefully but slowly, looking and listening, treading carefully. Always, I found myself pledging to return.

GREAT BRITAIN AND IRELAND

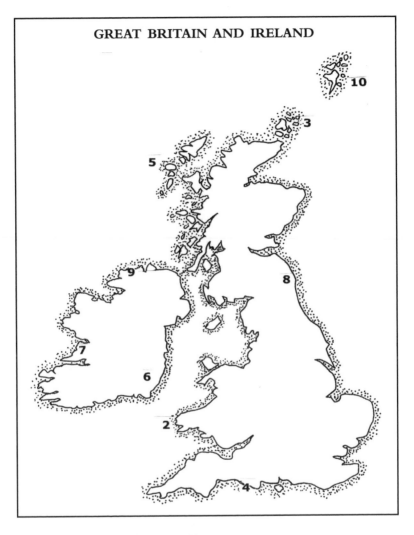

Locations by Chapter

1   INTRODUCTION

TO BEGIN IN THE MIDDLE – I recall an evening at the Rhyd-y-Creuau Study Centre in April 1974 listening to Evan Roberts, a third generation quarryman from the workings on Moel Siabod, in Snowdonia. After redundancy when the quarries closed in 1953 he became the first warden of Cwm Idwal nature reserve. Across these two phases of his life he learnt all there was to know about the natural history of his mountains. At seventy, and nearly blind, he had just returned from a trip to Switzerland to identify a previously unknown type of saxifrage – the rock-breaker. Only Evan Roberts, in the whole of Europe, could do that. He had recently, in winter, camped close to the sharp-edged ridge on Crib Goch with his grandsons – no doubt a wonderful tutorial. Evan Roberts was profoundly rooted in his landscape, his community, his language and a lost way of life. With slides that he knew by heart, he demonstrated his intimate knowledge of the mountains, in that delicious North Welsh version of English, to a small, spellbound group. Each of us realised, I think, that we had walked with a giant, an unconventional, self effacing hero. That mould, like so many, is broken now but we can still treasure its traces and each attune to its echoes for ourselves. We can savour our enjoyment of wild countryside and in our own ways edge towards some deeper insight and understanding.

Such moments inspire this venture. While wary of nostalgia we are still drawn to look back at the paths we have carved and hope to make some sense of the past. Few of us now have the secure roots of an Evan Roberts. That twist of unease runs through our much vaunted freedoms; we each have to find our own response.

I chose to seek out important friends from across my adult life, ranging in age from twenty four to seventy three years. I invited them to join me on short journeys to places I find compelling. We would

Moel Siabod – the quarries that were the workplace and
university of Evan Roberts for 40 years lie below the scarp slopes

Llyn Idwal from path to Devil's Kitchen. Evan Roberts was the
first warden of the nature reserve here, a special place
in the UK for mountain flora

take ourselves to some of the dramatic edges of Britain and Ireland, places still resonant of the ancients, communities with long histories and a proven capacity for survival, and coasts rich with wildlife. I knew we would see these landscapes differently and take our unique inspiration from them. I had enough confidence in these relationships to be sure that our serious purposes would always be infused with enjoyment and laughter. There would be time to reflect on our worlds, small and large, and on the different drumbeats to which we have marched. We could also weigh up how well our uniquely privileged generation has played its hand.

I assured everyone that these journeys were not to be feats of endurance, a message received with scepticism in some quarters. Nor would they be 'Last of the Summer Wine' meanderings through a second childhood. No voyages down hillsides in tin-baths or motorised wardrobes. My prospectus, happily, was well received.

These major strands of my enterprise deserve some fuller explanation. The ideas were intuitive but I have tugged at the roots that gave them their character. I think I owe it to anyone choosing to follow the winding trails of my journeys to fill in some of the clues.

FINDING FELLOW TRAVELLERS

I determined on a balance, some friends lost in the mists, others long term contacts, and my immediate family. There has to be some risk in renewing old friendships that are just safe and satisfying memories. Would the ingredients that once made the relationships work well still be active? I started from an assumption that these people, whom I had trusted and found sympathetic in the past, would have a shared instinct for this sort of exploration. Fundamentally, as adults, we change very little. I hoped that they would also feel that our friendships, whether formed in learning, growing up, sport, campaigning, mountain walking, working, holidaying or facing challenges together, still had vitality to relish. We could of course find we were relying on some idealised perception of a past that existed only in our deluded imaginations. Risks, we concluded, well worth taking.

Others here are long term friends, people I know well and have spent much time with, either at work or socially; but whose life stories I never quite managed to piece together. This would be chance to listen more carefully and tread some footsteps we always seemed to miss before. Some of their individual stories would merit a more extended telling. I enjoy travelling with all three of my close family. They each bring fresh eyes and interests; and they know how to prevent me taking myself too seriously.

We all wanted to travel responsibly, avoiding flights if we could. No-one argued for an exotic, ruinously expensive, or sun-soaked destination (some hopes!). Train travel for two proved grossly more expensive than use of an economical car. Anyway our destinations were often too remote for such choices. We managed usually to find modest but good quality accommodation. We tried to pace our ventures, chasing when we had to but slowing to a halt when we could. Please do not conclude from this new puritanism that the cast of this book are all deeply mean and miserable. The whole venture, even in the foulest weather, was great fun.

My cohort of chosen travellers comprised several nationalities and diverse careers. Undeniably my choices of people and places were self-indulgent. This project would be a wonderful way for me to reflect, to trace my own path and to enjoy places that inspire me, in the company of people I admire. It would be as much about the people as the places.

LOCATIONS, LOCATIONS, LOCATIONS

It feels important to explain my affinity to wild places and dramatic landscapes. Having grown up on the drab southern edge of London (yes, once upon a time, it did have edges), I retain vivid memories of discovering the countryside and my own ideas of beauty.

My mother and sister were evacuated during the Blitz to a remote farm in mid-Wales. We returned there for holidays a few times in the years after the war. To a five year old it could have been another planet. A steam train dragged its way through London's vast suburbs into a land green, rolling and empty. The farm was remote, without electricity, without neighbours. Heroic labour was essential just to make daily life work. Its barns were piled high with hay and straw. The real magic lay in two tractors, one blue and monstrous, the other red and boy-sized. I travelled endless imaginary miles at its wheel. I helped – or so I was allowed to believe – milk cows and churn butter of unique flavour. If ever I tasted it again that would be my own Proustian moment. We walked between huge grass banks rich with sweet wild strawberries, sometimes reaching the abandoned and overgrown farmstead, Pen y Bryn, even more evocative and sinister than the one we stayed in.

Bedtime meant a brave journey taking a flickering candle up an enclosed staircase to a bare room, shared with mice; scary enough in August, what must winter be like? One terrifying night a huge storm lashed the house. I sat by the window feeling its force, watching the oil-lamp flutter, simultaneously enjoying fear and security.

The Gaffer – as cheerful as any farmer of the time was allowed to be – grudgingly took a combine harvester on trial. At a stroke, and the emptying of a bank balance, the back-breaking labour of countless generations was brought to an end. His two sons, inevitably heroes to me, enjoyed great adventures, managing the livestock, driving those wonderful tractors, and taking a day off to taste the highlife of – whisper it – Aberystwyth. One of them could throw a tennis ball so high it disappeared from view before returning to his catch.

This was a dream world which long coloured my imagination and aspiration. I hated leaving it.

Then, at fifteen, I discovered mountains. I spent every school holiday from age nine to sixteen with one friend (still untraced) and we filled every day with indoor and outdoor games, sport, cycling, cinema, swimming and escaping to the North Downs to walk and wonder. JMF was a year older, more street-wise, adventurous and confident than his Sancho Panza, but it was a lasting friendship, strong on trust and common interests. We presented ourselves, on foot or cycle, at numerous spartan youth hostels, brushing out dormitories, polishing stairs, washing up for dozens in our turn.

The big adventure was Snowdonia, summer 1961. JMF had joined a school trip at Easter and was now set on leading his own expedition. I sat on the bench outside the hostel at Capel Curig, pulling on my case hard, ill-fitting boots, watching rain cascade across the sunlit face of Moel Siabod and decided that this was for me. It was a tough few days for a rookie mountain walker, then lacking the practised balance and co-ordination that usually ensure survival. Paths were paths in those days. No engineers needed yet to retrieve erosion. It was exhilarating to clamber over the extraordinary boulders to the precipitous summit of Tryfan, and to drag myself through penetrating drizzle to the gruesome café on top of Snowdon itself. As we arrived the clouds broke apart and the sun picked out ridges, lakes and valleys impossibly far below. As in a dream we caught the strains of a choir performing evocative Welsh hymns –Cwm Rhondda and Cymer, Iesu, Fi Fel'Rydwyf – while we fed sandwiches to gulls hanging in the wind. The Salvation Army had joined forces with the mountain worshippers.

The evening air was intoxicating, with views to those distant summits mesmerising we innocents. Some types of magic, happily, change little over time. Legend has it that Sherpa Tenzing Norgay, on his first view of Snowdon from Capel Curig, asked 'How far to base camp?' A passion had been spun that would never leave me. Islands and wild coasts followed from there.

My interest in wildlife reached lift-off on the Isles of Scilly in summer 1970. It was near the end of the nesting season. The

Tryfan rising above Ogwen valley near Capel Curig

enthusiasm of boat skippers explaining their rich environment was contagious. The beginnings of new skills and delights identifying and understanding birds and animals sat well alongside my other interests. Gradually I also started to make more sense of the historical layers in our landscapes, trailing in the wake of the WG Hoskins and Bill Rollinson. Perhaps I should have tried to progress to specialise as a true twitcher or as an expert on stone circles or fungi; but I marched to my own tune in the wilds, a jack-of-all-passions, with history writ large.

A UNIQUELY FAVOURED GENERATION

It is hardly contentious to suggest that my generation, the post-war baby boomers, was uniquely privileged; but I knew we would find many different angles on it all.

The lives of the three preceding generations had been devastated by unspeakable suffering in two World Wars. A large majority were haunted by poverty, hunger, epidemics, minimal education, and unemployment. They scarcely expected to reach retirement and were physically exhausted if they did; more threat than promise. The years beyond 1945 were austere, but as children few of us knew hunger. Progressively we became wealthy beyond the dreams of our parents and grandparents, not always in monetary terms but in the choices available to us. In education, healthcare, food, child-bearing, employment, travel, technologies, material well-being, sexuality, cultural and racial diversity our inheritance became freer and richer.

In enjoying such prosperity we blundered through some massive challenges, often in collective denial. We allowed the gulf between obscene wealth and abject poverty to grow ever wider. At a minute to midnight we realised that our well-being had been achieved through profligacy with the planet's natural resources. The generation given so much time to play and to learn suddenly found itself confronted by the immeasurable threat of climate change. Prosperity became our opiate. Now, we had to wake up.

It often feels that we have been mere observers to the great dramas of our age. But we shed real tears of joy at the end of apartheid, the Mandela miracle, the fall of the accursed Berlin Wall and the collapse of Soviet autocracy, and a real end to the long disaster in Ireland. We are able to engage with the nations of a lost Empire as equal partners. We grudgingly accept that the EU has bound up centuries of wretched wars. Even we in the chorus play a part.

So how do we measure up against the heroic generation which threw off the depression and appeasement to win the agonisingly long battle with Nazism? Would we have been equal to such challenges? We grew up in the shadow of their certainties, some of which failed the test of time, but somehow held society better than we do now. We have battled our way towards some crucially liberating secular values – gender and racial equality, respect for difference, greater freedom of expression and behaviour, accountability for power and open justice. These all remain fragile under pressure; but they are still the essence of the victory over Fascism and Stalinism. For all its shortcomings perhaps our legacy will not look so threadbare if such values are sustained.

An agenda for wet evenings and sunny cliff tops.

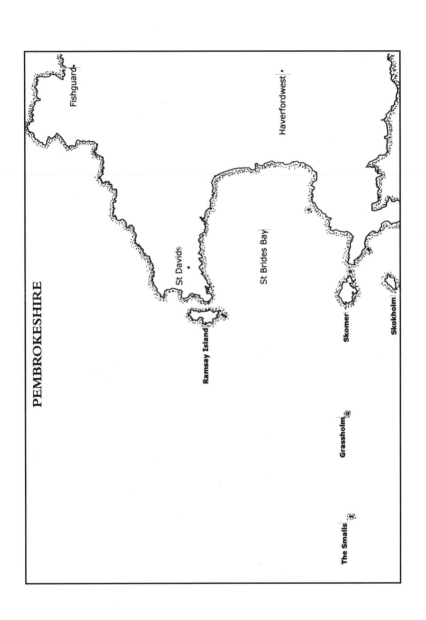

2   PEMBROKESHIRE, ST. DAVID'S

IT WAS A POINT OF PRINCIPLE for me to seek agreement with my conscripts about the timing, location, accommodation and activities of our adventure. Helen, my daughter, agreed readily enough to a few days away just after her final examinations at Vet School; but she adamantly refused to negotiate. It was all down to me. She was 'all through with thinking'. My occasional tentative suggestions while she was in revision mode were consistently deflected. In short 'Whatever'. Pembrokeshire? 'Fine'. So long as it was different from her current labours. She deserved and achieved success in the finals, so finding the best break to refresh her afterwards felt like an important challenge.

Helen and I had journeyed before, apart from holidays and camping trips. When she was twelve, slumped at home with flu, she could manage nothing better than to watch a Test Match. After so many hours she was hypnotised and became a cricket fan. There followed the occasional day at Old Trafford, Trent Bridge and Headingley. Then I spotted that the Trinidad Test fell in her February half term. The match was a terrific contest, which England won by an inch on the 5th day, with Mark Butcher digging deep for victory. We relished seeing Ambrose and Walsh in their awesome pomp. Our seats were immediately adjacent to the players' route onto the field so fair-haired Helen collected autographs and smiles from her heroes. The joyous atmosphere in the crowd at the Queen's Park Oval bubbled throughout the five days regardless of the cricket and the result. Then three days on the beach in Tobago before returning to cold foggy England and more chemistry lessons.

Nearly two years later it was Port Elizabeth and South Africa, another tough five day match in front of a similarly happy crowd. The PE youth brass band blasted its full five tune repertoire incessantly, eventually joining forces with England's Barmy Army to dance away the final hours of the drawn game. We also made a couple of safari journeys. Helen (just about) put up with my endless 'embarrassing' conversations with folk on their hopes and fears for the new South Africa. The almost universal sense of optimism, even in the face of desperately difficult social problems, was both humbling and intoxicating. The image that brought a few tears was our first visit to the beach. Less than a decade before this would have been a whites-only preserve; now it belonged to everyone, including a young mother, in full burqa, knee deep in the sea playing with her three little children. One small paddle for woman – one giant leap for humankind.

FOLLOWING THE WINDS

I did not promise sunshine and happy, singing crowds in south west Wales. Indeed my record in attracting wild weather is notorious and this week added to it. The tip of Pembrokeshire is usually windy of course but throughout our stay the boatmen on whom we were depending had to make fine judgments as to whether they should go to sea at all. When they did it was wonderfully rough and their seamanship extraordinary. No doubt they relish such challenges, and it does help to make them a living.

Travelling across Wales has for centuries been famously tortuous and dangerous. The modern road network, with a lot of new bridges, has cast a veneer of comfort onto the legend. The labyrinth of roads that leads incidentally into Pembrokeshire provides many delights – beautiful rolling hills populated solely by sheep, occasional, unpretentious villages, and enticing seascapes. Progress is still very slow so there was plenty of time to relish it all.

Coastal Pembrokeshire has its distinctive character, relatively wealthy and diverse. English language predominates over Welsh, unlike so much of rural Wales. The familiar English place names often bear little relationship to the original Welsh versions, either by sound or translation. Abergwaun has improbably become Fishguard, Aberteifi is Cardigan, Trefdraeth Newport.

Language has been a fundamental strand in the troubled history of Wales and England. In the centuries before the waves of Anglo Saxons drove Celtic communities into their western strongholds, Welsh dominated the vernacular culture of these islands. It was largely

Welsh sheep pens – artistry in stone

unwritten but elaborately rich in its visual, emotional and imaginative range. The English of the invaders was deemed, by contrast, to be 'the thin language' by the Welsh. When Edward I became King in 1272 it is estimated that over forty per cent of his subjects spoke Welsh or Gaelic. The governing elite still spoke French and recorded much in Latin. Edward's campaigns against the Scots and the Welsh, renowned for their military power and the enduring castles, took the obliteration of the Welsh language as a primary objective. This campaign of cultural suppression lasted for centuries. Even in the 1880s Westminster deemed it necessary to ban the Welsh language from schools. Pupils were routinely punished for using their family language in school. Like Cornish it was destined for oblivion until an astonishing revival in the second half of the last century – hard won and still rather begrudged in England. Perhaps it is time to celebrate this extraordinary achievement, even if the road signs do baffle us.

Happily St David's itself translates directly from the Welsh Tyddewi. The city, famed as the smallest in the UK, still comes as a surprise. It seemed little bigger than many of the places we passed on the way. In fact it is, by population, smaller than many villages across the UK. The

Evening surfer near St David's Head

St David's Cathedral towering below the city

cathedral lies below the settlement and is far from imposing until you venture beyond the tiny city square. It occupies a classic monastic location. The scale is out of all conventional proportion with its urban attachment. It may not compare with the beauty of Durham, Lincoln or Salisbury but the elegance and extent of the site bear testimony to its local and national importance. Its lofty spacious interior is handsome and light.

It contains the tomb of Gerald of Wales, author of the first known book about Wales. Gerald was of mixed stock – son of a Norman baron and a mother from the Welsh aristocracy. He became an archdeacon, thwarted by Canterbury in his ambition to become Bishop of his beloved St David's. He was directed in 1188, already in his forties, to tour Wales to recruit support for the Crusade. He planned his 500 mile trek from Hereford to broach some of the steepest mountains and most dangerous rivers as well as visiting many of the major settlements. He was unusually tall and a strong horseman. His remarkable endurance was not rewarded with vast numbers of recruits for the Crusade but he did become arguably the first and finest medieval British travel writer. His intended audience was other Latin scholars across Europe; his eventual readership has been infinitely broader. Gerald lived into his mid seventies, producing seventeen books – an incredible achievement for that era. He found his final rest in the cathedral that he loved.

The winds picked up and the temperature dropped on that first evening. No boats could leave harbour. Our first foray into the catering options was dispiriting. The sign outside the beautifully located coastal pub proclaiming 'Best Whitby Scampi' should have served as a warning that we were set to enjoy some fruits of the freezer rather than St Bride's Bay. The place was crowded and cheerful enough to deceive. The meal confirmed our worst fears. A prolonged sunset behind a troubled sky, over a wild beach made for a stunningly beautiful compensation.

SHEER WATER

Tuesday morning brought a veritable deluge. We enjoyed an hour at Strumble Head, peering vainly onto a grey sea and imagining ragged waves into porpoises, but the search proved unproductive. We retreated to Fishguard, arriving to ankle deep water in the car park. The narrow pavements provided perfect sluices for water hurled from passing traffic. A hand-written board advertising a home-baking coffee shop at fifty metres promised sanctuary (down river); but it was a mirage, long since closed. St David's, we had already noticed, has an excess of coffee shops; perhaps the Tourist Board or some such agency could promote some redistribution in favour of Fishguard. Or maybe it is too busy laying plans for a fleet of arks.

We took refuge in one of the many small, warm, cafes in St David's, leaving it considerably steamier than we found it. Helen decided that part of her post-finals therapy might lie in a large jigsaw, so we raided the National Trust shop for a characteristically kitsch 1000 piece puzzle. It became a personal challenge to finish it before she left on Friday.

The skies cleared but strong winds continued throughout the afternoon. A phone call confirmed that a boat would venture out beyond Ramsay Island to the Bishop and Clerks Rocks later on. The small vessel with a dozen passengers left the landing stage below the reassuring Life Boat station with amazing power. On the OS maps Ramsay Sound looks innocent enough, even sheltered. The reality is very different. Underlying troughs and a massive tidal race create powerful, spectacular rapids that have claimed many lives and also attract the most accomplished (if slightly unhinged) canoeists. I started to appreciate the strength of our boat's engines as we steered away from the maelstrom. Better – or for some, worse – was to come.

Ramsay ends in a series of angular rocks and islets. I assumed we were heading beyond these when quite suddenly our skipper pointed the vessel head on towards an impossibly narrow, V-shaped gap, flooding wildly with huge waves from both east and west. With the engine idling he left his wheelhouse to share with us some of his vast expertise about the birds nesting around the island. Invaluable as this was, I suspect I was not alone in hoping that he would not leave the boat untended in such waters for too long. These fears were needless. With a style borrowed from the Dukes of Hazzard, he took the boat at full power through the imaginary gap, while we all breathed in. We progressed around the exposed, western side of Ramsay, pausing close in to watch the various nesting colonies on the cliffs. The fulmars took pride of place, their distinctive stiff winged flight and delightfully haphazard landings compelling to watch. Their notorious capacity for projectile vomiting a uniquely foul smelling liquid made for a good story as the boat tumbled in a heavy sea. The thought of elite climbers being targeted by fulmars and having their costly clothing irretrievably soiled brought winces and smiles in equal measure. We beat a further improbable track out to the Bishop (a lighthouse) and his Clerks to see the puffin colonies.

Then it was back to Ramsay Sound for an extraordinary climax to the evening. Manx Shearwater nest on Skomer and Skokholm Islands at the southern end of St Bride's Bay. Each day they fly north in their thousands to feed offshore beyond Ramsay Island. They are difficult to see because they travel in the half-light of dawn and dusk, and fly close to the water. When the seas are high however they return early, presumably because of the additional hazards of the journey. We now had the rare privilege of seeing at close quarters an unimaginable torrent of shearwater swarming south, a flickering ribbon just above the water. A breathtaking sight – a marine fantasy. Our skipper talked us quietly through this event, concluding with an ominous amen: 'They say that if you can see the shearwater flying south through Ramsay Sound, then you really should

Fulmar in conversation on their nest

16

not be out there'. His words hung in the air as the silvery thread of birds faded into the growing darkness. It was a theatrical conclusion to an exhilarating trip, made possible only by marvellous seamanship.

SUN, SAND AND HORSES

Another wild night was followed by a dry, windy morning which gave us chance to potter along a stretch of the northern coastal path, trying to make sense of some unusual industrial remains and to discover the guide book's 'best remote beach' in the region. The ruins, which included a kilometre of a railway bed and some huge brick hoppers, turned out to be evidence of granite crushing. Who but the Victorians could have contemplated crushing granite? Further on the famed beach a few hundred feet below was windswept and deserted but nonetheless impressive. We investigated the track down but withdrew in recognition that this beautiful and extensive series of coves was facing directly into the westerly winds. Best viewed from afar, we decided.

More therapy for the new graduate came in the form of horse riding on the sands of St Bride's Bay. The image of horses galloping along the edge of the surf may be a photographic cliché but in the swirl of a summer afternoon it still conveyed some magic. The subdued light and the sea spray conjured up a medieval backdrop for the event – a dozen horses careering to and fro delighting in an uninhibited chase.

After a meal at an excellent bistro in St David's we fell again for the great Strumble Head porpoise hoax. Be in no doubt that this is an exceptionally lovely point from which to watch the sun disappear into the Irish Sea; but the legend of porpoises swarming happily in the tidal race around the headland remains unproven – for us at least. Meanwhile the clock was still ticking on that jigsaw so it was back to our roost for some serious business.

TO THE SMALLS

The winds relented enough next morning for another boat to venture out from St Justinian, this time in search of whales and

17

Helen, horse and surf on St Bride's Bay

dolphins as well as birds. This was advertised as a demanding trip lasting three hours and heading a long way out towards south east Ireland. Ten brave souls took their places on a small but substantial boat and we proceeded at a ferocious speed towards Grassholm, a four acre rock, which in earlier times was used to graze sheep. It beggars belief that the need for pasture was so great as to lure shepherds and their hapless flocks to such an exposed knot of grassy rock. The thought of rowing out to the island with a boat full of livestock stretches the imagination. Today the place belongs almost exclusively to a massive gannet colony, which rendered the whole of the island's eastern aspect white. I never tire of watching gannets soaring, acrobatically diving, jostling to land, courting their mates and just resting. They are singularly elegant, powerful and dignified. After due pause, our boat resumed its westerly course at maximum speed despite an increasingly hostile sea.

Water was now crossing the boat from all angles and at all heights. Helen and I were feeling smug in our head to toe waterproofs, although conversation was reduced to brief shouts at close quarters. When the boat slowed to scan for whales, the random power of the sea, pitching the little vessel even more severely, took control. By this time four of the ten passengers were grimly attached to buckets; the other six were doing their best not to notice, which in so small a tilting space was difficult. The condition of the four was not helped when we reached the Smalls outcrop and its desolate lighthouse. By comparison it made Grassholm look like Manhattan. As the boat rolled every glimpse of the light set it at different and wholly improbable angles from the vertical. Not that the view from a bucket varies much anyway, I suppose.

The Smalls is the third point of a triangle of lights which guard the access to the whole Pembroke peninsular and its harbours. It is terrifyingly isolated and exposed, perched on a barely visible reef. Above the light is a wide, sinister brim of steel mesh on which the maintenance helicopter lands. The Smalls is notorious for a gruesome tale from around 1800. Two keepers, known to be at odds, took up their tour of duty. One of them died. The other, fearing he would be accused of murder, hung the body outside the light. Ships reported a ghostly apparition swinging in the winds. When a relief crew arrived,

The Smalls Lighthouse, a mere 30 kilometres from St David's, originating in 1770s, rebuilt in 1861; a chilling sight.

the lone keeper was found to have lost his mind. The Smalls was, from then on, always crewed by three men, not two – until automation, as everywhere, removed the need for such heroism.

We beat a course around the light searching for signs of whales or dolphins, but without success. We moved north, then west again in vain. There were birds aplenty, especially shearwater and even arctic skua, but the main purpose of the venture was to be thwarted until we were safely in the calm waters of Ramsay Sound. There at last were the elusive porpoises, wheeling away with abandon. Even the famous four gingerly raised their heads from the buckets to enjoy the show. They started slowly to return from their near death experience, faces slowly shading from green to puce. A vote of six to four declared the journey a great experience; it did us no harm to be reminded that the wildlife is not there to perform on our behalf. The image of the Smalls lingers even now in my imagination; and of the shepherd retrieving his flock from Grassholm.

REALITY

A return to the cabin to dry off, shower and to complete the jigsaw project was abruptly overtaken by the dreadful news of the London bombings which killed dozens of people and injured hundreds. We sat watching in disbelief and with few words at first. It was hard to switch from our essentially light-hearted, storm-tossed sojourn to absorb this indiscriminate carnage. We, like everyone, were jolted from our assumptions by it all. Until this, the day had been so exhilarating and had left us with much to reflect on. All perspective was now lost.

Maybe Helen expected me to be able to explain and interpret what we were seeing, but I had no inclination, or capacity, to rationalise it; thirty six dead, seven hundred injured, recurrent images of mangled wreckage. The victims were of all races and creeds. Could there be a more cosmopolitan target than London's public transport? Could there be a surer way of harming ordinary folk while leaving the powerful and wealthy untouched? Could the fanatics really have decided that Muslims living humdrum lives in London had so betrayed their creed as to deserve obliteration? The 24 hour news channels, which were created to be able to respond to such crises, seemed to flounder with endless, repetitive description of the scenes, but little informing analysis. Over the next 48 hours they, and we, recovered some perspective, without shedding the sense of horror. I suppose for Helen and me these will always be the Pembrokeshire bombs.

A GRAND FAREWELL

We treated ourselves to one last sunset over on St. David's Head. The height and time of the tide were just right for a wildlife finale. Through binoculars, in fading light, we watched porpoise scything through turbulent water and, again, the unmistakable silvery pulse of the shearwater rush hour, hurtling south to Skomer and Skokholm. This was a moment of real surprise and excitement. The winds had not really abated for the whole of our visit but we had gathered in some wonderful experiences.

And so, early next day we left, skirting the Preseli Hills, making a thoroughly mistaken attempt to land in Aberystwyth, which was full.

Venerable common seal looking for some easy fish

21

We wheeled home over the endless, empty hills of mid Wales, a cosy contrast to the exhilarating wildness of the Pembrokeshire coast. Helen's sights were now rightly fixed on the first steps of her career. For me, a new resolution – to visit Skomer and complete the cyclical saga of the mesmerising shearwater.

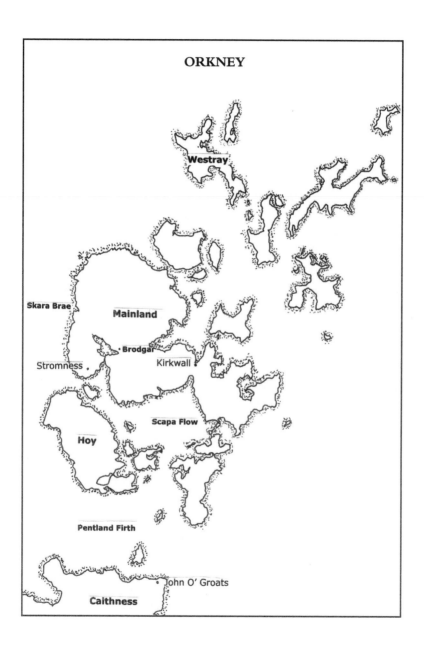

3.   ORKNEY

OLD HANDS — NEW HORIZONS.

DAVID AND I had not met for over thirty years. Neither of us had been to Orkney and it was high on our wish list. We set out with high expectations.

David and I met in the 1960s at Atlantic College, a newly created, residential, international sixth form college in a castle perched on the cliffs of South Wales. In the disorientation that inevitably afflicted sixteen year olds away from home for the first time, new friendships kept us afloat. David and I had enough in common quickly to forge a strong alliance. By temperament we were both easy going but tenacious. Both of us arrived at AC from grammar schools, on LEA scholarships. Our family backgrounds were modest, with no previous experience of higher education. We both still wonder whether we were ideal material for the AC project but gave it our best shot and took much from the experience.

A few shared, random, memories may serve to convey the flavour. David and I found ourselves in the same beginners' German group, bewildered that the whole enterprise was conducted at a searing pace in German from minute one. Such practice has become conventional now but in the 1960s it felt disturbingly revolutionary. We both wanted to ask if we were in the right group but lacked the vocabulary and courage to do so.

The college's location, and the inspiration of its founders, led to the creation of coastal rescue services, on which every student spent at least three half days per week. This came as second nature to some but it was a foreign, rough terrain to others. David contrived to stay on (comparatively) dry land, rehearsing abseils, climbs and winching manoeuvres on the crumbling Glamorgan cliffs. I trained in three seasons in the surf at Southerndown and just about made it as a lifesaver. We all had to be first aiders. How far all this was character

24

building, as intended, is difficult to say but it did stamp us with a new awareness of interdependent teamwork and some exposure to risk.

Competitive activity took second place but the newly formed college football team gave us early, familiar respite, though few victories. We played on a tilting strip of pasture on the cliffs, with evil winds sweeping in from the Bristol Channel and indignant evicted sheep for spectators. David occasionally scored goals while I conceded rather more, but we travelled the Welsh valleys and the towns in good heart. We were even feted as an exotic, international team by some schools (until they saw us perform).

On Sundays a few of us cycled a few windy westerly miles along the coast to help out at a home for blind children, selflessly sharing duties with the agreeable female staff.

David and I were in the same (brand new) timber house/dormitory blocks, where personal qualities inevitably emerged more dramatically. He and I tended to stand back in some amusement watching or assisting the star turns. We recall vainly trying to rescue Gavin, a wild, impetuous, delightful Scot, from wrecking the place in a drunken rant one Saturday evening, carrying him as far as possible from the scene of his disaster – a shattered plate glass door. Rod, a tough, cheerful, worldly-wise eighteen-rising-thirty year old rogue, was in love. He persuaded a caretaker to risk his job by briefly lending him a Yale gate key so that he could pursue his amour. At lights-out he started slowly but noisily to file a copy of this key on his locker, to the great delight of eleven sleepy students. David and I discovered the limits of our influence with him. The conventional sanction in college was log-cutting – four for a first offence, doubled for a second or for failing to turn up. Rod's accumulator has prevented him from ever going near the college again.

Apart from a very occasional meeting, the last of them in the mid-seventies, David and I had gone our separate ways until I made contact late in 2004. We agreed in principle on Orkney in September 2005. I visited David for a weekend in August to negotiate our plans. We were confident that by temperament, interests, humour and view of the world we would be able to renew our friendship without pretence or evasion. And so it proved. I could not have hoped for a better start to my venture into the deep past – personal and historical.

APPROACH TO ORKNEY

We were both enthused by the prospect of Orkney. These islands are, quite simply, marvellous – despite some huge grey skies. Maybe I brought a greater historical understanding to it all than David but his keen interest made for an excellent balance. His focus on whisky, both in theory and practice, took me into new territory. Our shared observations of the ebb and flow of people and happenings in Orkney kept us smiling. The week also worked because we found a happy pace – readiness to put energy into our chosen visits but with space for photography and pondering, times out for coffee, snooping and just standing aside to watch.

David flew from London into Inverness, incidentally in the company of Charles Kennedy and his family. Within three months Kennedy had to resign. You may consider this mere coincidence but David later admitted, under the influence of a little Highland Park, to be working under cover for Welsh intelligence in Buckinghamshire. The official papers will reveal all in 2035.

We drove to Gills' Bay for the ferry across the awesome Pentland Firth to St Margaret's Hope. Gills' Bay, to be frank, lacks glamour. Its harbour wall is buttressed by the hull of a well rusted oil tanker but it provided an efficient service with little fuss. Dolphins crossed the bay as we waited. Restless, noisy oystercatchers fed and panicked nearby and a flock of dunlin swept around in spectacular acrobatics, glistening in the evening sun.

The ferry does daily battle with powerful tidal energies generated by the meeting of the North Sea and the Atlantic. The vessel held its own while crossing these maelstroms but it was chastening to hear the engines grind slow and to feel the ship slew sideways. How did the early venturers to Orkney manage to paddle these crushing tidal waters? Even when the channel was narrower, before the ice sheet melted to its fullest extent, the junction of two great seas must always have been uniquely formidable. Orkney had compelling attractions for hunter-gatherers and would-be settlers. The islands are easily visible and alluring from the mainland. They offer rich soils, lush pasture, sheltered seas for fishing and large natural harbours, an enticing prospect in contrast to the mainland's northern shores. The prevailing climate in the early Neolithic period was gentler and warmer than now. Even so the Pentland Firth is a graphic reminder of the courage, skills and tenacity of our ancestors.

Our first acquaintance with Orkney was a journey north to Kirkwall in deepest darkness, crossing the formidable Churchill Barriers, narrow causeways between once isolated islands. We circled the town like an aircraft searching for a runway before homing in on our large but well concealed guest house. It served our purposes well enough but functioned eccentrically, like a benign Fawlty Towers. Only three of the twelve rooms were occupied, which maybe disturbed the usual smooth routines of the house. More probably it was just cheerfully dysfunctional. The manager had an ill-disguised alcohol problem and a propensity to mislay his specs at crucial moments. Like Basil, he relied on a 'Polly'- in this case the cook – to hold it all together.

SOLID CAPITAL

Kirkwall was next day blessed with blue skies, which gave its solid and well maintained harbour facades a distinctive elegance. The main street boasted numerous locally owned shops; only Boots and Woolworths

Pentland Firth looking towards John O' Groats. Treacherous, turbulent waters where North Sea meets the Atlantic

seem to have intruded from the UK identikit high street. We momentarily assumed the stone flags which lined the narrow street as a form of pedestrianisation. They are of course the ages-old road surface both in Kirkwall and Stromness. The town's most prominent feature, unmistakable from land and sea, is the imposing St Magnus Cathedral, regarded as the finest remaining Norse building in Britain. Inside it is wonderfully light and majestic. St Magnus was a truly noble figure of legendary proportion and found fame as a martyr. One aspect of his story that struck us was, unfortunately, less heroic. He married and apparently took an immediate ten year vow of chastity. His bride's views are not recorded.

Our first impressions of Kirkwall endured –a busy, prosperous, and confident community which enjoys its tourist incomers without being over-dependent on them. Increasing numbers of large cruise ships overwhelm it in the summer months. Some signs of economic fragility are evident on the edges of the town centre, with a few boarded-up shops, but by most comparisons Kirkwall looks resilient. One shop seeks to sustain the sturdy well-being of the townsfolk with a poster urging

Kirkwall waterfront

Baker's window in Kirkwall

them to "Say Aye Tae A Pie" above a picture of a young boy happily munching on a pastry wider than his face. Hide your tears Jamie Oliver.

A SETTLED COMMUNITY

Historians are tentative about Orkney's earliest human activity. There is still so much evidence to be gathered. Hundreds of locations remain to be excavated. The age of sites can now be reliably fixed by radio-carbon dating and pollen analysis. Maybe advances in DNA processing will yet reveal more precisely the origins of the earliest settlers. They found rich prospects in Orkney: animals for hunting, good soil for crops and livestock, salt and fresh waters abundant in fish, workable building stone, peat and driftwood for fuel. They created stone circles of perfection; at least eighty chambered burial sites, and the sublimely preserved settlement of Skara Brae. In truth every corner of these islands reveals evidence of its prehistory. We had time to sample only a few sites.

Part of Skara Brae and the Stones of Stenness have been conclusively dated to around 3000BC, an astonishingly early point in the progress of these British islands towards settled communal living. Close by stand the huge, nearly complete stone circle of Brodgar, and the most celebrated of the stone chambers, Maes Howe. Each significantly predates Stonehenge. The visual impact of these four sites took us both by surprise. Orkney's vast skies, across a gently rolling, treeless landscape, with seas to all sides, are stunning enough. The stone circles, poised perfectly in the folds of verdant pastures, their secrets still intact, focus the eye and the spirit. The vision and collective energies of the societies that created these structures tested our inadequate imaginations.

Maes Howe is an underground burial chamber of sophisticated design. It dates from about 3000BC, earlier than Stonehenge and the Pyramids. The inch-perfect alignment of the entrance tunnel with sunset on the winter solstice confirms its elemental purpose. Maes Howe will retain most of its secrets forever. It fell into disuse (or different use) after about six hundred years. When the Norse raiders broke through the roof in around 1150AD they took or destroyed almost all evidence within. The Norse runes neatly carved into the stones describe some robust activities invariably attributed to Vikings. These were discovered when the chamber was re-opened and excavated in the 1860s. There are cryptic references to treasures. But what 'treasures' could a stone-age culture have left to excite rapacious Norsemen? This is a moving and mysterious place, much more than a tomb; surely a focus for ceremonials and communing with tribal ancestors.

Religious and cultural sites often bear indecipherable clues. By contrast Skara Brae, like no other, reveals its story explicitly. The settlement is contemporaneous with Maes Howe, although not adjacent to it. The village is incomparably intimate, with stone furniture, even ornaments, securely enclosed in tall circular walls. The families might have just left these dwellings – but for the disappearance of their roofs. Originally sited – in about 3100BC – some way inland, the settlers had

Ring of Brodgar, huge perfect stone circle

Stones of Stenness,
oldest Neolithic structure adjacent to Brodgar

easy access to fresh water and to the sea. They were surrounded by rich pasture and fertile soils. The village flourished, and was extended, and probably rebuilt, before being abandoned around 2500BC. The treeless landscape meant that building had to be in local flat-bedded stone – hence its longevity. The intrusion of the sea (as levels rose) closer to the settlement may explain the relocation. Sea spray will progressively have affected the crop cycle and the quality of the pasture. The village subsequently succumbed to inundation by sand and disappeared under dunes until the mid 19th Century – a mere four millenia.

A massive storm then tore into the dunes and revealed parts of the houses below. Almost certainly this was the culmination of erosion over the centuries. In all probability a swathe of the original settlement had already been sacrificed to the sea. The difference by the 1850s was that the science of archeology was well enough established for the exposed site to be investigated. The village was robust enough to withstand Victorian excavation and remained to be skilfully restored a century later. The whole site is now open to the

Village of Skara Brae – family dwelling, furnished, last occupied 4500 years ago

elements and to the public. A sea wall protects it directly from the sea but the adjacent dunes are being seriously eroded. Skara Brae will be at serious risk over the coming decades unless its status as a world heritage site produces more extensive defences.

The interpretation centre for the site is exceptional, including a convincing replica of a single roofed hut. The path across to the village itself traces a simple timeline conveying very effectively just how deep into the mists you are treading. Is it really possible that this stone furniture, the artefacts, the hearths, the beds, the little curving corridors, even the ornaments, really were the fabric of people's lives five thousand years ago? The evidence here is beyond dispute and requires little imagination. It is detailed, even mundane; but we gasped as we began to absorb its significance.

Taken together these major Neolithic sites are awesome. We both admitted to spine-tingling reactions in all four locations. That there are so many such sites*, scattered across these little islands, conjures a much greater challenge to the imagination. By pre-historic standards, Orkney must have been positively congested; certainly it was wealthy. Probably like many visitors, bemused by these unique places, we paid too little attention to the remains left by subsequent societies in Orkney – especially the Brochs, sturdy circular stone fortresses developed in the last centuries BC, and the scant evidence of five hundred years of Norse settlement. These islands deserve more time and more visits. You need to experience the flow of the seasons, and many more of the seventy two Orkney islands, to stumble towards any real comprehension as to how human life has made its peace over five thousand years with such a demanding but exalting environment.

GREAT EXPLORATIONS

In Stromness it is the dark waters of the harbour, as much as the meandering, stone-flagged streets and alleys of the town, that bear the secrets of history. This was the great harbour of the Viking longships.

*In summer 2007 an excavation revealed important evidence of an extensive village community close to the Ring of Brodgar and contemporary with Skara Brae.

It became the last secure touching point of most voyages aimed at exploring the Arctic seas and to establish the elusive North-West passage to the Indies. Stromness lies due east from the southern tip of Greenland and the Davis Strait which guards the entrance to Hudson Bay. So in the centuries of courage before an understanding of longitude was captured, the port offered opportunity to set a westerly compass for North America. Stromness became the harbour for whalers, fur traders, sealers, and explorers. This was the port that serviced the Hudson Bay Company (HBC), established in 1670 with licence to exploit the frozen north of America for trade. Login's Well, in the centre of the town, provided fresh water for countless voyages; and here was the last chance to stock with fresh fruit and vegetables as a guard against scurvy.

It was also the birthplace in 1813 of John Rae, doctor turned surveyor and explorer with the HBC. Rae, as an outsider who dared to challenge the prejudices of the Victorian establishment, has contemporary significance. His personal aptitude as a skilled Arctic traveller was unequalled in terms of distances covered, speed, hardships and hazards overcome, coast surveyed and understanding of the native peoples. He set out to learn from and deploy Inuit technologies and skills (an approach now promoted passionately to our own generation by Ray Mears). For instance he built ice-houses rather than having to rely on tents or huts. He mapped hundreds of miles of rivers and shorelines around Hudson Bay and its hinterland. Yet in his lifetime he found as much notoriety as celebrity.

In 1853 the British government commissioned Rae (among others) to trace Sir John Franklin's fateful North-West Passage expedition which had left England in 1845. The following spring Rae met with Inuit travellers who bore artefacts and relics that were unmistakably from Franklin's ships, the Terror and the Erebus. Through a trusted and capable interpreter, Rae interviewed about twenty Inuit individually. The dreadful story of Franklin's men dying either near their ice-trapped ships west of King Williams' Land or on desperate treks south, gradually took shape. The Inuit independently reported evidence of cannibalism among some of the refugees. Rae knew that other expeditions, and many lives, were still being risked to find survivors of Franklin's team. So he decided to return to London as soon as possible with the news, rather than over-winter again in order to seek first hand, incontrovertible, proof.

Rae knew and trusted the Inuit. Alas he was not an accomplished writer. He might perhaps have been less forthright when he conveyed the awful intelligence about the fate of the expedition and the evidence of cannibalism. Lady Franklin, a formidable, well-connected and combative woman, bullied the establishment to denounce Rae. Charles Dickens lent his powerful pen to her cause. The assault on Rae bears comparison with the character assassinations so beloved of today's tabloid press. As an Orcadian he was an outsider. His unchallengeable achievements as the leading Arctic surveyor and explorer for the Hudson's Bay Company were discounted.

Rae had chosen to rely on the word of 'savages' (ie the Inuit). To respect the Inuit was intolerable; to admire them was treason; and to believe their evidence about the fallibility of English officers and gentlemen merited banishment to outer darkness. The British establishment was shortly to reel before the impact of Darwin's Origin of Species (1859). The authorities were rallying desperately to defend the basic tenets of Victorian society and of Britain's global roles: the moral and racial superiority of the governing classes and the infallibility of Scripture. Rae was crushed and swept aside. First hand and forensic evidence subsequently vindicated him.

The relics and the stories presented by Rae were at least accepted as proof of the demise of Franklin's expedition. By attrition, and in defiance of the evidence, Lady Franklin managed to persuade the authorities that her husband had discovered the North-West Passage. (This would be akin, for instance, to claiming that Scott had beaten Amundsen to the South Pole). A grandiose memorial to her husband near Pall Mall bears testimony to her powers. As so often the verdict of history, for the time being, belonged to those with the pen and the power. Rae, the outsider from Orkney, admirer of the Inuit, was edged from the page. The map-makers, however, were not fooled. Rae Strait, the final piece in the jigsaw of the North-West Passage, is a stretch of sea east of King William Island first surveyed by the doctor from Orkney. Amundsen, no less, followed the Rae Strait in 1903 to complete the first ever passage to the Pacific.

THE BOY DAVID

Between our plunges into deep history and wild landscapes in Orkney, David and I reflected on the world our generation had inherited and the one we are handing on. We both benefited from the educational opportunities that moderately bright children enjoyed after the war. We thrived in our primary school classes of nearly fifty pupils – sadly not everyone did. We both won our grammar school tickets and were academically successful but with quite different experiences. His was a benign environment typical of the proud tradition of education in the Welsh valleys. David has a high respect, even affection, for his teachers. Mine was a London boys' school, routinely and unnecessarily brutal and inexcusably programmed to fail many of its lower stream pupils. Such pupils would be stars in today's comprehensives but they felt alienated and used their intelligence to make teaching them a misery. Sport, a few friends and a few enlightened teachers rescued the place for me.

We identified an important common strand however. Most of our teachers had been shaped by their roles in the war, in uniform or otherwise. They knew right from wrong. They had fought for their values and won at a terrible price. Without the heroism of that generation our lives would have been unimaginably worse. This gave them a justifiable certainty about their roles and beliefs as teachers in this new era.

Necessary respect for authority and for day-to-day rules was too often taken to extremes. I recall one hapless individual who was spotted at lunch using his knife and fork 'the wrong way round'. Interrogated publicly, with over a hundred silent, cowed spectators, he confessed to the misfortune of being left-handed. He was briskly taught the error of his ways. Routines, regimentation and clan loyalties dominated school life, leaving little room for imagination or creativity. The benefits of this were the strong basic skills and narrow specialisms we lucky ones emerged with. We were, at least, well drilled. Too much talent was needlessly wasted however.

David and his peers enjoyed greater individual encouragement and recognition than I recall. Neither of us however remembers taking any key decisions for ourselves. The railroading into streams by aptitude occurred without noticeable consultation. Subject choices at fourteen into or away from the sciences were made for us, which of course constrained our scope after sixteen. University was assumed to be the worthy destination for those who could. Academic achievement was exalted above everything (except sport). We were pawns on our schools' chessboard. Neither we nor our parents questioned their right in exercising such judgments on our behalf. Careers information was plentiful but no education supported it. That infamous interview inflicted on Jimmy Casper in 'Kes' was no caricature; schools knew best. So David and I can both celebrate the more generous and enabling attitudes adopted towards our children by schools and society. Not to be taken for granted.

The two of us arrived at Atlantic College by intriguingly different routes. David's headteacher called him in and advised that he would be an ideal candidate; so David cheerfully did as he was told. I happened to be listening during an assembly when the Head read in desultory manner a notice about some college in south Wales. My mood must have been alert for an escape plan. I collected the papers, discovered the deadline had already passed and quickly sought advice outside school. Before I awoke I was being interviewed for an LEA scholarship and was offered a place. Such initiative on my part was unusual; it even came as a shock. The college and the LEA, I suspect, had not been inundated with applications.

Two years at Atlantic College made a world of difference to both of us. It recruited students, even then, from over forty countries, all, as I recall, on public scholarships. Its purpose was visionary and ambitious, framed largely by ex-officers committed to preventing another generation from stumbling into war. Their guru was Kurt Hahn. The logic was that if you brought young people from all over the world to spend two years living and learning together prior to university, you would be contributing in some rather ill-defined way to 'international understanding'. In retrospect the phrase sounds almost quaint. The regime was quite spartan, egalitarian, secular and fixed on service – coastal rescue mainly – rather than competitive sport. It was physically demanding and, at first, intellectually bewildering because the teaching demanded participation beyond my experience. The teaching staff included many talented and ambitious characters who knew how to challenge and inspire but also how to conduct skilful internecine warfare in the staffroom.

David's favourite memory is of a genuinely admired teacher, who returned from a cliff rescue training course determined to demonstrate the latest abseiling technique. This involved proceeding face downwards, rather than the conventional backwards descent. The rest of the anecdote tells itself. Said teacher landed with force face down on the grass in the inner courtyard of St Donat's Castle. Recovering his composure with a characteristic hitch of the trousers and a hearty laugh, he advised the students not to try the new method just yet.

The images remain vivid. We both carry a deep sense of appreciation that AC pulled us out of our respective ruts. The two years were intensive and original. We indulged in some nostalgia but also asked the harder questions that take us back to AC. We were gratified between us to make some more sense of it.

We both identify strongly with the secular values that have now become dominant in British society – equality of opportunity, respect for difference, a balance of individual rights with responsibility, and the primacy of the rule of law. These are easy phrases disguising profound transformation of attitudes and of laws. In Britain we grumpily take our democratic institutions and social stability for granted. We have, overall, become more comfortable with our cultural diversity. Our good fortune leaves us vulnerable now to the terrorism of fundamentalists and the aggrieved. So this generation has as much cause to remain fixed on defending its values as those who resisted earlier forms of Fascism.

David and I fastened very much onto the idea that individuals should be enabled to take their own decisions and to live with the consequences. So we are more inclined to help someone reach their own choice than to tell them what to do. David is a purist on this. Whenever we approached an awkward choice at road junctions, he would explain earnestly that the decision must belong, in the end, to the driver not the navigator. I should, apparently, try to learn from the experience and grow as result. He seemed nobly prepared, for the sake of his principles, to accept the probability that he might be invited to walk home.

SCAPA FLOW

On a beautiful Orkney morning we turned our focus to matters naval, a dominant feature of life in the islands in the 20th Century. In both world wars Scapa Flow, the huge sheet of water protected by the islands, served as the British fleet's home base. The fleet sailed from here to confront the Germans at the indecisive battle of Jutland in 1916. A few days later HMS Hampshire set off from the Flow for Murmansk. An hour later it struck a mine and sank with the loss of almost all hands, and of Lord Kitchener, Minister of War, who was on a mission to Russia to fortify their engagement in the conflict. (Lloyd George should have been on board but cancelled because of a crisis over Ireland).

In November 1918, when the Germans surrendered, their High Seas Fleet was disarmed and escorted to Scapa Flow. Seventy four ships remained at anchor for the duration of the Versailles peace negotiations until June 1919. They were prevented from communicating directly with the interim German authorities and, as the months passed, increasingly fell victim to rumour and speculation about their fate. As Versailles was completed, the word spread that the German representatives might refuse to sign such a humiliating settlement – in which case war could have re-started. The idea seems absurd: the allies had partly de-mobilised, the Americans had withdrawn and Europe had lost millions to a winter flu epidemic. But isolated in Scapa Flow for nine months the German fleet knew only fear and honour.

Its commander, Admiral von Reuter, concluded that his ships might be commandeered by the Allies. On 21st June 1919, while most of the British fleet was away from the confines of Scapa Flow on manoeuvres, he gave the order to evacuate his men and to scuttle the ships. Lacking explosives, the engineers had to turn to other means of flooding their vessels, which was a slow process. The British fleet returned at speed and tried to cut the anchor chains of the German ships so that they would be washed ashore. Nearly thirty were salvaged in this way. The rest sank, to varying depths. About half were subsequently salvaged. The remainder lie thirty or more metres down in Scapa Flow.

Until recently only well-equipped divers have been able to see any of this wreckage. Despite our Atlantic College credentials neither David nor I could dive beyond about three metres, so we felt some sense of privilege to watch from a boat as a remote controlled (and very expensive) submersible camera sent back pictures of the SMS Dresden. It is still intact but lying on its side, thirty metres below and shrouded in weed – a macabre but compelling memorial to a moving and melancholy episode.

HMS ROYAL OAK

One of the British ships involved in limiting the damage of von Reuter's decision in 1919 was HMS Royal Oak, a newly commissioned vessel. In October 1939 this same ship was left guarding the radar station on Orkney's East Mainland while the rest of the fleet went on exercise. A German U-boat, commanded by a trawler skipper who knew the waters too well, penetrated the defences of Kirk Sound and entered Scapa Flow, but found the fleet absent. It homed in on HMS Royal Oak, sank it, killing over eight hundred men, and escaped. Had the fleet been on station in Scapa Flow the losses would almost certainly have been disastrous. Just six weeks into the war it was a demoralising and terrifying event for Orkney and the nation. It presaged the terrible losses inflicted by submarines in the long battle for control of the north Atlantic. In Berlin the sinking of the Royal Oak was gleefully celebrated. Churchill subsequently authorised the sealing of Scapa Flow's eastern channels with stone and concrete blocks. Italian prisoners of war were obliged to assist in building the Churchill Barriers. From May 1945 these became permanent causeways with roads linking four islands to the East Mainland.

HMS Royal Oak is marked by a buoy as an official war grave, its loss commemorated every year by Orcadians and the Navy. The barriers are impressive both as feats of engineering and as a testimony to desperate times early in the war. They have an eerie beauty as well, even though they comprise thousands of two metre concrete cubes (If only the Turner prize had been on offer in 1945 !). Alongside them lie the wrecks of freight vessels sunk in the First World War and left in place as obstacles. The Italians left Orkney a curious memorial of their own by converting one of their corrugated iron huts into an elaborate chapel, to which many ex-prisoners have returned over the years. It has recently been impressively restored.

David and I were laying some ghosts here. We both knew of Scapa Flow's crucial importance in our naval and national history but we had never chased down the detail of events nor had chance to explore the visible evidence of its noble, tragic story. We saw it from different angles, both in sun and in that more typical glowering grey merger of sea and sky, an expanse of water like no other; and as stirring in its own way as the sites of the ancients.

THE OLD MAN OF HOY

We had chosen to visit Orkney in September even though it is the point of the year when birdlife is at its least compelling. The nesting season is over. The teeming cliffs have fallen almost silent and turn again from white to green; and the autumn migrants have not yet started to arrive. I had however reckoned without Hoy's distinctive

Great Skua, piratical scavenger of the islands

offering. It is a rugged and mountainous island out of character with the rest of Orkney, and a major breeding ground for the Great Skua. Significant numbers remain through the autumn.

It is difficult to think of any redeeming features to offset the Skua's well earned reputation as a vicious, ruthless, piratical and parasitical villain of the high seas. They are large, agile birds which steal their food by mugging gannets and other skilled fish-catchers. I had not experienced their gentler side, which turned out, of course, to be the product of low cunning. A clutch of them followed our little boat across to Hoy in the same benign manner of gulls searching for scraps. When we halted they dropped to the water in coy imitation of ducks on a municipal pond. With wings folded they appear much smaller than expected. Most of the boats on this stretch of water catch and discard fish; in Skua lore they are therefore worth pursuing. Skuas are obviously not quite bright enough to distinguish tourists from fishermen. The best they could hope for from our little crew was a leftover sardine sandwich.

Four of us joined this little boat in Stromness. It was quite a feeling to sail out of this particular harbour glancing back at largely the same rugged profile of buildings that John Rae and countless others knew and longed for. Our skipper for the afternoon briefed us well on safety, with reassuring advice as to what we should do if he were to be swept overboard. Laughter covered our unease.

The Old Man of Hoy is a rough hour by sea from Stromness, although this day was not extreme. The stack stands improbably at one hundred and thrity seven metres on the westernmost corner of Orkney, with towering three hundred metre high cliffs as a backdrop. A circle of basalt at the foot of the stack, resistant even to these turbulent waters, explains its existence; but if you feel compelled to climb it I suggest, for two reasons, you do not wait too long. First it looks very vulnerable to further erosion. Secondly, your condition might just worsen beyond the point where you are allowed out. No Mountain Rescue service exists on Orkney and the RAF advises climbers not to expect assistance if in difficulty. It is not, apparently, a technically difficult climb but its remoteness and exposure make it a very special challenge. In the nesting season the close attention of fulmars, with their uniquely vile projectile vomit, beyond the scope of

The Old Man of Hoy with small fishing vessel in attendance

all known cleaning systems, adds to the fun.

David and I both recall the televised climb of the Old Man in 1967 when Jo Brown and friends spiralled with improbable ease to the cap; so again it was a place fixed in our imaginations and wonderful to see at close quarters.

David's day became even more memorable when he discovered on Stromness quayside a stall selling the finest chips in the world. He has laid plans to return.

A VENTURE NORTH

On Sunday we set off for Westray, over an hour's ferry journey to the north, passing several other out-islands. Watching Kirkwall disappear as we sailed under leaden grey skies was revealing. It became just a ribbon of rooftops set in vast swathe of sea, glowering sky and low slung, green, treeless hills; a magnetic harbour in a huge, beautiful, emptiness.

For anyone of philosophical or poetic bent, do go to Orkney.

A chance conversation on the boat with a visitor from the Scottish west coast near Skye helped make a bit more sense of what we were seeing. Everywhere the huge, lush meadows here are populated with impressively large and healthy livestock – muscular and impassive sheep, and several varieties of cattle. They spend up to six months under cover but provide, as they have for millennia, a rich resource for the local community and its trade. It is part of folklore that an Orcadian is primarily a farmer who fishes; a Shetlander is the reverse, first a fisherman, incidentally a farmer. The obvious contrast with the west coast of Scotland is that Orkney is overwhelmingly grassland, with hardly any trees and, significantly, little or no bracken; so it is a paradise for sheep and cattle. The weather is wild but temperatures rarely extreme; and drought is but an abstract idea.

What makes Orkney so distinctively different from mainland Scotland? Is it the strength of the Norse influence that shaped life on the islands for 500 years? Orkney has no fjords or mountains but among some of its young people the handsome Nordic features are traceable, at least to the imagination. Orkney escaped the anguish of the clearances. In Caithness, by contrast, tenants were driven north to an impoverished existence along the coast, where farming was tough and learning to fish even worse. Orkney does not bear such scars. Language, with all its cultural associations, may be a factor. Gaelic never took root here. Viking and Pictish influences on place names are strong. The Orcadian tongue has not survived the layers of invasion, but a proud, unshakable sense of identity undoubtedly has. Its ingredients are a rich theme for research.

We had been advised to think of Westray as just one huge farm, allowing for the fact that it has over three thousand cattle, even more sheep, and only seven hundred people. It greeted us under a blanket of grey, with cool breezes sweeping mountains of cloud from the west. With little forewarning, in early afternoon, it slipped its dark shackles and for a couple of hours a massive canopy of blue sky transformed the endless meadows. The sheltered shoreline of Pierowall Bay is another large shallow harbour which afforded safe anchorage for the Viking longships and which has sustained whitefish and creel industries even into the 21st Century. We idled in the sunshine, watching snipe, dunlin and oystercatcher plying the tide line.

The modest island hotel lays credible claim to being the finest fish restaurant in Scotland. Investments by the Highland and Islands Enterprise board and the EU support a café and tourist guide business as well as a small youth centre. Orkney has received less support from the EU social and economic initiatives than much of Scotland as it is less impoverished. We reflected that the struggle of any isolated community to adapt and survive must be similar wherever they are located. Westray's folk could be forgiven if they reacted to mere tourists as misplaced intruders but they offer a convincingly warm welcome, with drivers waving, passers-by greeting us quietly but wholeheartedly, and the services attentive. In conversation, they seem contented and firmly attached to their remote way of life. We could not imagine what the island might feel like in the dark days of winter; there is no way really to understand such places without taking time to watch the seasons unfold.

As we joined the short queue for the return ferry early on Sunday evening, another piece of the Orkney jigsaw fell into place. In those last few moments before the ferry was due to leave, a series of car headlights sped down to the quay. A dozen or so young people aged fourteen plus from Westray were starting their school week, catching the ship to Kirkwall, where they are resident. During the day we had noticed little groups of them enjoying each others' company at different places, including the café and the shore. Now they were subdued, some sleeping on the benches in the ship's lounge, others huddled around tables in quiet conversations, keeping each others' spirits up as dusk turned to dark. No doubt, like all social routines, such partings become familiar; but it made a sombre end our day. For us it recalled those long, cold Sunday evenings at Atlantic College. These young people and their parents face the dilemma of generations of island Scots (if they will permit such description): where do they seek their futures – in the confines of their own communities or in the small wide world now so easily open to them?

David meanwhile was engaged on the ferry, by chance, in a challenging conversation with a Scottish research student whose knowledge of his national history was comprehensive. His style of conversation resembled an intensive university tutorial, so that, on the trigger of a given location, person, or outrage he would proceed both to inform and to interrogate. As a Welshman, David was able of course to sidestep the direct responsibility that we English are, not unreasonably, deemed to have for almost every misfortune in Scottish history. David enjoyed the encounter but I sensed he was relieved we were not on the eight hour trip to Aberdeen. I spent most of the journey watching from the open deck as the shadows of land and sea disappeared into the blackness.

HIGHLAND PARK

The most northerly distillery in the UK happened also to be the first I had ever visited. David is a more seasoned whisky tourist. We two were the sole members of the group escorted by our guide, Poppy, around the amazing process, through the malt floors, the peat fired treatment of the grain, to the sophisticated distilling equipment and measurement, and the hall of casks. We contrived to ask ever more fiendish questions but Poppy knew her stuff. It was a joy to come across a manufacturing process where quality prohibits significant change. If ever I should find myself paying £300 for a bottle of thirty year old malt whisky, I will be consoled to know that it has been produced by people deploying age-old skills, largely without the intervention of new technologies or chemical agents. Just think what has happened to our beer. Whether you drink whisky or not, raise a glass of something to its genius and its purity, and to the sons and grandsons who labour patiently to make it.

BROKEN PRIDE

In the mid sixties David's native Welsh valleys wore a very different aspect from now. Then, apart from producing the best rugby players, the South Wales coalfields were still vibrant and proud communities. Steel, petrochemical and other heavy industries added to a sense of hard-earned well-being. So we fell to discussing the disasters that had, since the 1980s, created such a deep depression across the valleys.

We shared our sadness at the decline and at the difficulties of reversing it. David is optimistic about the growth of small businesses, the museums, the bookshops, the investment in regeneration and leisure services; but these were such distinctive communities, so brutally broken, that repair could take generations. The harshest manual labour had shaped the character of these communities, just like fishing villages. They held to their own brand of religion and invested proudly in education. So, widespread unemployment was doubly destructive, undermining family and social relationships as well as depriving people of the dignity and routines of work. That sense of hopelessness connects into schools, where even young children adopt the negative expectations of older relatives. What sort of household is it where only the children have any reason to get up in the morning? And all, of course, compounded by the geographical isolation of the valley towns.

As on Westray, families and young people are torn between an intuitive loyalty to their communities and a dreadful realisation that the only way to achieve a secure living is to move away. Perhaps we should match our Orkney journey with a passage across the Welsh valleys. Another day.

TO THE WOODS

We left Orkney on a grey wet day perfectly designed for farewells. The Pentland Firth did its turbulent best to drag the ferry anywhere but south. We were nonetheless duly returned to Gills' Bay and the long road to Inverness, this time in the dark and in relentless Scottish rain. So it was not until the next day, driving further south, that I realised the joy of seeing forests and mountains again. Orkney has its own special appeal but it is still a stark landscape to the unaccustomed eye. Fortunately beauty is not competitive and, like the greatest whisky, can be made finer by blending. We both came away mightily impressed with Orkney and the richer for renewing a mislaid friendship.

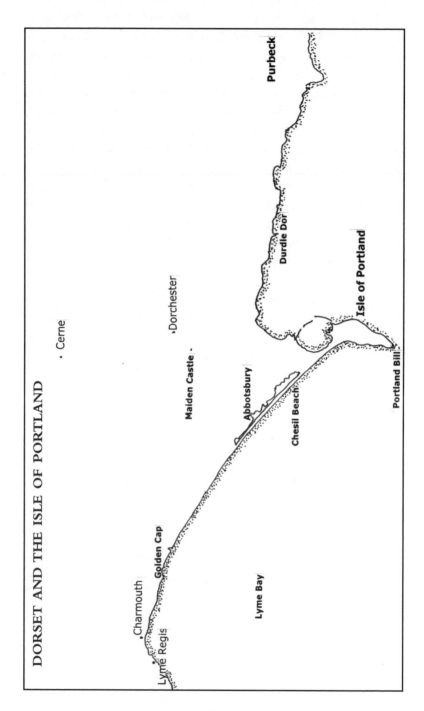

DORSET AND THE ISLE OF PORTLAND

4. DORSET AND THE ISLE OF PORTLAND

THIS VENTURE diverged from my prospectus – a trio, not a pair, journeying through one of the wealthiest counties in England, rather than the rugged outposts I had signalled. We had been good friends at university and a three-way reunion after thirty five years seemed the obvious outcome. Dorset was the agreed destination. It proved ideal for our joint interests. The Ancients stalk this region, through all the layers of its history. Its island, such a contrast to mainland Dorset, and a lethal magnet for shipping, is renowned for its exquisite architectural stone.

DRAMATIS PERSONAE

Norbert arrived in Oxford from Germany to study Sanskrit as a preliminary to taking on a leading role in the Catholic Church in India. His vast age (viewed from the barely post–adolescent condition of the rest of us) and his status as a priest might have kept him aloof. Not Norbert though. He was obviously a man of serious intent but totally without pomposity. Very tall, fair haired, with a wicked, self deprecating sense of humour and a slim athletic physique, he was widely respected. He graced the college football team as an agile but roving (some said absentee) centre half. His intellectual prowess, even in a second language, was obvious and he was the focus of many a vigorous discussion. In 1967 the Papal Encyclical 'Humanae Vitae' re–affirmed the Church's stance on birth control. As a non-Catholic I had no idea how anyone could justify the cruelty of encouraging population growth in countries – not least India– beset with poverty and famine. Norbert held the line about the importance of enduring values over short-term expediency, but I sensed his unease. Then a leading British Catholic intellectual, Charles Davies, left the priesthood to marry. We heard him speak about the crushing consequences of his decision. Norbert identified with Davies' trauma but his own commitment seemed unshaken. I retained a strong impression of Norbert's integrity and strength of character.

Norbert disappeared from my radar within a couple of years. From somewhere I collected occasional fragments of news. He spent a few years in India, working to bring a new generation of Indian Catholic priests closer to the needs of the poorest in society. Then he returned to Bochum University in Germany. The next, happy intelligence came in the mid 1980s: Norbert had left the priesthood and married. Some twenty years on, as I stitched this venture together, it took only a few moments on the internet to discover this distinguished theologian and inter-faith visionary. A few e-mails, phone calls and months later, I travelled to Wurzburg, wearing a smile of anticipation all the way, to meet up with my renegade priest and his family. For me (and I hope for them) it was lovely weekend. It re-affirmed for me the idea that, fundamentally, people change little even over decades. All the qualities I recalled were still evident. He had left the priesthood without a breach of his faith or purposes in life. Now he seems fulfilled in his marriage to Birgit, a delightful person and a sympathetic psychotherapist. They are the cheerfully harassed parents of an energetic son and daughter in their late teens. Norbert's academic reputation is such that he has been in demand in Germany to interpret other faiths in the wake of 9/11. His sense of humour has also survived. So these really were many happy returns for us.

We set about negotiating the journey. Norbert was characteristically enthusiastic, though he has travelled the world too much. His one request was that we try to involve Bill, whom he remembered fondly. Otherwise he would go anywhere, anytime – family and professional commitments permitting; which narrowed down the options to just a couple of weeks over the next six months.

Throughout our time together at Oxford, Bill was the easiest of company in a community stacked with many intense, ambitious students. His range of interests, his sense of humour, and his unfailingly generous nature put him on good terms with many, whether wrestling over some impenetrable essay, pulling a superbly co-ordinated rowing eight to many narrow defeats, or just enjoying being a student. We enjoyed, sometimes with Norbert and others, several hill walking ventures together and have remained in touch. Initially Bill worked in a Law Centre. He is now the senior partner in a law firm and a mainstay of a local dramatic society.

I cannot think of Bill without acknowledging the agonising challenge he and Wendy have faced in bringing up two sons afflicted with Friedrich's Ataxia, a painfully degenerative condition. Becky, mercifully, is fit and well. They have done everything to ensure that the boys, now in their twenties, enjoy as full and happy a life as possible. Both are very intelligent and engaging; they have progressed to university, travelled widely and devotedly followed Arsenal for years. Andrew now sadly has almost lost his sight. Their handicaps require constant care but both have determinedly achieved a degree of independent living that does them great credit. The strains on everyone in the family are unimaginable. I was delighted that Bill readily agreed to join us for a few days away, so long as family demands did not intervene.

My original, mistaken, notion had been to go to the Hebrides. We quickly realised that the remoteness would difficult for Bill and an excessive journey for Norbert. My second idea took us to the Isles of Scilly but the emphasis on wildlife was too narrow for our shared interests. The solution was Dorset, rich in its layers of history, with a coast of rare beauty and significance for our understanding of the earth's history; and the Isle of Portland, suspended by the slender thread of Chesil Beach. It was a good match to our expectations.

STARTING AT STONEHENGE

We met at Stonehenge, a convergent point for our routes to Dorset and a first for Norbert. Of all ancient sites Stonehenge is peerless in its immediate visual impact. It is a complex construction, the product of many generations. In spring 2008 the first major excavation within the circle for half a century is to be conducted. By deploying the latest scientific techniques the dig should create greater certainty about the sequence and dates of its creation. The latest research, as of now, puts the placement of the inner Sarsen stones at about 2500BC. These were brought two hundred and fifty kilometres from the Preseli hills and seem to have been of enduring significance at the site probably for their alleged healing qualities. The wood henge and the circular ditches surrounding it go back into the ill-defined realms of pre-history. How did a dispersed society still reliant on stone tools and elementary agriculture formulate a collective ambition to create such a temple? What beliefs compelled scores of generations to devote themselves to recreating the site over again? The surrounding plain carries innumerable burial chambers and evidence of processional routeways, marked by further ceremonial gathering sites. If Stonehenge is to yield more of its secrets, the territory around it may have more to reveal more than the stones themselves. I am intrigued by its precise location. Why was this site chosen rather than any other on Salisbury Plain? It is certainly not on the highest point, but the site is conspicuous from every local approach and the processional avenues all rise towards it. Just another dimension to the mystery.

In the adjacent Kenet valley a parallel, but evidently separate, undertaking bore the creation of Avebury Rings, Silbury and a similar hinterland of avenues and burial sites. Taken together these seem to reflect a transition of Neolithic beliefs and priorities. Communal burial

Stonehenge – the smaller Sarsen 'blue' stones from Preseli hills form the inner circle and are thought to be the focus of ceremonials.

mounds here and elsewhere (such as Maes Howe on Orkney) invariably stand in prominent positions overlooking tribal territories, perhaps expressing the continuing involvement of ancestral spirits in shaping the fortunes of the living. Orientation to the summer or winter solstices suggests worship related to the seasons. Subsequently more elaborate stone circles, sometimes contained within a henge (ditch), seem to reflect a more sophisticated reading of the rhythms of moon and planets. In short, ancestor worship yielded priority over time to astrological intelligence.

Stonehenge is a place for profound questions; but much simple pleasure derives from just being there. It is of course a tourist honeypot but it attracts a degree of reverence denied to many historical sites. The endless crocodile circulates gently in a roped avenue around the Stones, which at least allows everyone an uninterrupted view. An incessant stream of road traffic passes close by but somehow is not too intrusive. English Heritage is campaigning for a quality visitor centre, which is surely needed, and for a re-routing of traffic away from the site, but the costs look prohibitive. EH also want to present the site in its wider context, especially by way of the Avenue along which our ancestors, it is assumed, approached the great arena.

Norbert was hugely impressed with Stonehenge both for its visual impact and for the unfathomable questions it poses. We badgered him for a truly German perspective. Spying a stone out of vertical he conceded that the site was 'probably durable but somewhat lacking in precision'. Has he borrowed irony from the UK or is it home-grown? In the EH shop we tried in vain to persuade him that the pop-up model of the site would make a sophisticated souvenir.

Like most visitors we gave Stonehenge just an hour, wondering if we could ever return for quiet access to the Stones themselves. Then to complete our pre-Dorset preliminaries we struck south to Salisbury.

The famed spire, though close by, cannot be seen from the city centre; we wended our way through narrow streets to catch our first glimpse. Again we rather insulted another of Britain's finest buildings by rushing our visit. Several generations committed themselves to fulfilling the dream of this glorious cathedral. I wondered whether they were in some way influenced by the presence, just a day's walk away, of the greatest pagan temple at Stonehenge. Were they trying to eclipse its allure with that slender lofty spire? We were struck by how much the simple elegance of the Close adds to the impact of the Cathedral.

WELCOME TO DORSET

Dorset itself began for us with a visit to a former colleague of Bill's in her lovely 16th century thatched cottage near the coast. The living room had lots of nooks and doorways with scarcely a straight line, vertical or horizontal, to be seen. It took on the slightly surreal air of a stage set. Phones rang, doors were knocked, and surprise characters, including an affable local estate agent, sped in with interesting news and exited stage left. Bill called his office and discovered that no-one (including him) had been paid for April. We rehearsed his escape plan. Hadn't Reggie Perrin's bid for a new life started on a Dorset beach? We duly made our own exit to a guest house perched just above the west Dorset cliffs. A calm seascape, lit by the dropping sun, provided a reassuring end to the day.

This was the first time we three had been together since 1968. It seemed months rather than decades ago. Our exchanges were fairly intense and to us, at least, often very funny, disappearing along extravagant tangents. Few stories reached a conclusion. A good start to the venture.

LYME REGIS AND THE JURASSIC COAST

Lyme Regis summoned us with several voices. Edward I endowed Lyme, an ancient settlement, with the honour 'Regis'. The harbour, created by the medieval Cobb, served fishing, trading and naval fleets, and played its role in the Armada. A century later, in June 1685, a self-proclaimed Protestant champion, the Duke of Monmouth, landed an invasion force of eighty men west of the Cobb. Defeat followed near Bristol. Judge Jefferies, at the Assize Court in Dorchester, administered a terrifying justice, which took a dozen Lyme citizens to the gallows by the beach where Monmouth had landed. The town was already in decline and languished until the virtues of sea-bathing were discovered around 1760.

Literary associations – among them Jane Austen, Henry Fielding, Thomas Hardy, John Fowles – have contributed to its colour and character. If only Meryl Streep had been parading moodily along the Cobb or the Undercliff, I could have conjured such a picture for Norbert.

I associate Lyme with a dreadful day in 1993 when a group of teenagers from Plymouth were taken out for an initial canoeing experience on the deceptive calm of the Bay. Four were drowned as an off-shore wind prevented the party from returning to safety. The activity centre managers were imprisoned for negligence. For once the frequent sentiment that 'lessons must be learnt' had meaning. An effective enquiry generated a campaign, led by David Jameson, MP for Plymouth, for legislation to regulate Outdoor Centres and Activites. Regulation, in this case, worked well because it had the enthusiasm of all skilled, responsible practitioners behind it. For some though Lyme Bay will always be a tragic place.

The Lyme Regis we arrived in wore a disrupted air with extensive coastal defence reconstruction in progress. In simple terms the town has been sliding into the sea. My main informant, a local dog-warden, had already lost a large slice of his garden in a land slip. The whole frontage of the town – perhaps a kilometre – is being reinforced with deep-driven piles, stepped concrete walls, new groynes, and tons of imported gravel. From this ugly chrysalis is emerging a well designed and sympathetic new sea front, including a sandy play beach. A drama of much greater consequence than those conjured by Lyme's novelists is being played out among the JCBs and cranes on its shoreline.

We shifted our attention eastwards to Charmouth, whose cliffs are also under lethal assault from the sea, to the misguided delight of the fossil hunting community. These shores played a crucial part, through Mary Anning, born in 1799, in first unravelling the significance of its rich fossil bearing strata for geology, science and for religious belief. The almost incessant clattering of tiny hammers bears testimony to the compelling nature of the search for trophy ammonites and belemites. Like Lottery players, the hammerers pursue the fantasy of an astonishing whole, reptilian, skeleton. For the unsuccessful hunter there is always the shop by the shore, stacked high with specimens from all over the fossil world.

Bill and Norbert took to the beach, seized by the challenge of this simplest of amateur pursuits. Norbert surprised us with a Pythonesque moment by declaring that he felt inspired to create a new sect, under the 'Fossile' banner, with himself as spiritual leader, me as his chief representative and Bill as his sole, unfortunate follower. The principles of the new sect emerged haphazardly over the next few days, mainly at moments when our one true leader was at a loss for rational thought. Most notably pebbles were to be held sacred and not to be eaten during Lent.

In theory, the South West Coastal path strikes up the cliffs from Charmouth towards Golden Cap, at one ninety metres the highest point on England's south coast. Sadly the sea has torn a huge chasm in the path and will be back for more of these fragile cliffs each year. We retreated inland to Stonebarrow for a gentle, talking pace, walk up to the Cap. In bright sunshine we fell, rather incongruously, to exchanging stories about the impact of wartime on our respective families. This was new territory for us, safe enough within our friendships, but still poignant, even disturbing.

BOY NORBERT ON GOLDEN CAP

Norbert's family ran a prosperous manufacturing business in Essen before the war and had avoided the worst ravages of the 1920s currency collapse. They became compliant but unenthusiastic citizens of the Nazi regime. They lost everything, except the site of their factory, in air raids in 1944/45. Norbert's mother was then evacuated with her children to the countryside. He recalls seeing a huge American armoured division on the skyline trundling relentlessly across the area, which was now virtually defenceless. Nearby a solitary German tank commander chose to mount token and futile resistance. This drew two hours of US heavy bombardment onto their adopted village. The roof of their house was sliced off.

When the gunfire subsided Norbert's mother, evidently a feisty individual, set off from the cellar to retrieve her valuables from the bedroom upstairs, taking little Norbert with her. An American soldier was already in the room, about to loot it. He directed his gun at Norbert's mother who proceeded, with great presence of mind, to persuade him not to steal her personal treasures. Somehow a moment of terror became a dialogue and the beginning of a tentative, post-war friendship. A few weeks later Norbert's family received a food parcel from relatives in South West Africa – until 1919 a German colony. His mother called Norbert over and told him to hold out his hand. He took from her a mysterious dark tablet – his first ever taste of chocolate.

On top of Golden Cap, a wonderful viewpoint along the coast and inland across a quilt of meadows and hedgerows, we were overtaken by a mirage (unless it was those mushrooms we had collected). A group of llamas arrived from the east. They wore harnesses and were accompanied by a cheerful group of young people, who could hardly be confused with Peruvian tribesmen. Bill went to negotiate peace. This exotic outing was a wedding celebration, the animals borrowed from a local sanctuary.

The day turned from spring to summer as we descended to Stonebarrow, with the first powerful warmth of the year. Without any real excuse, except to provide Norbert with another initiation into British culture, we descended upon a cottage selling cream teas in a beautiful shady garden. Norbert looked quite aghast at the idea of tea with cream in it and was bemused to see the huge, very light, scones and bowls of clotted cream and jam arrive. However he set to the challenge single-mindedly while Bill and I lapsed into a 'where are they now?' interlude. As we left, regret already mounting, we saw a notice proclaiming this (quite plausibly) to be 'the best cream tea in Dorset'. We briefly wondered who had undertaken the research behind this claim and which re-hab centre was looking after them.

ABBOTSBURY

The pendulum swung back to spring, with a hint of winter, next morning. We were treated to an ethereal view of Chesil Beach and the silhouette of the Isle of Portland from an elevated point on the coast road. Bill had signalled in advance that he found Portland forbidding and sinister, and would prefer not to visit it. He has always had a serious interest in architecture so I felt sure he would be drawn to the story

Llamas on Golden Cap for a wedding

View to Chesil Beach and Isle of Portland

of Portland stone when the moment arrived. However his unease was real. We therefore re-designated it the 'Isle-with-no-Name'. I mentioned it once but I think I got away with it.

Our initial destination anyway was Abbotsbury, an exquisite village of thatched cottages, winding streets and, disconcertingly, lots of people in mediaeval dress. We made for the Swannery, a place of great calm. The huge colony of swans, alas in early May without cygnets, copes equably with the hordes of human visitors. The swans claimed this ideal site on the richly stocked lagoon behind Chesil Beach, long before the Benedictine Monks adopted it – another fragment in Dorset's extraordinary history. Swans rarely congregate in large numbers for more than a few days so the behaviours at Abbotsbury are very unusual. Even when sitting on eggs the nesting pairs tolerate close scrutiny from their curious daily observers. Chance for everyone to be an Attenborough for a couple of hours. Immature swans seem well tolerated. We saw no more aggressive conduct than in the average primary school playground. A fascinating habitat- a place for all seasons; but my return will be timed for when the young have hatched.

Nesting swans at Abbotsbury, tolerant of human hordes at close quarters. A swan sanctuary for many centuries

MAIDEN CASTLE

Our journey now turned inland under heavy skies. We did not allow enough time for the stretch of countryside across to Maiden Castle but in truth its significance would require a pilgrimage on foot. This is ancient Dorset, haunting and atmospheric, much celebrated by Thomas Hardy. Around this ridge of hills and across to Studland are scattered hundreds of Neolithic burial mounds, long barrows and Bronze Age (2200–650BC) round barrows. So here is another heavily populated tribal territory, just sixty kilometres south of Stonehenge, inviting comparison with Neolithic Orkney.

Maiden Castle is reckoned to be the most extensive Iron Age hill fort in Western Europe. Its steep, lofty ramparts are hugely impressive. Given the scale of pre-Iron Age settlement in the area the fort almost certainly dates back many centuries before its refined completion. The visual impact on approach is memorable. The vast, flat meadow in the centre of the fort is dull by comparison, an impression not helped by the forlorn state of its resident sheep. The Romans took possession of this formidable site and developed Dorchester, scarcely a glance away, as their urban, military base. Look towards the unpromising outskirts of Dorchester from the ramparts and the eye is drawn to yet one more solitary long barrow, assiduously preserved amidst the ploughing, an assertive reminder of whose land this originally was.

The association of Goethe to Maiden Castle is little known outside the tight circle of Bill, Norbert and myself. Bill was pleased that Wendy, recovering from an operation, had been able to turn her attention to an OU assignment on Goethe. Recognising the breadth of Norbert's intellect she sought his advice. The conversation began as we left the car and raged unabated for the whole visit. My interventions were minor – but quite crucial in preventing Bill and Norbert from reaching any conclusions. I had half listened to Melvyn Bragg's 'In Our Time' on Radio 4 about Goethe three months before. Half listening to 'In Our Time' is ill-advised. The density of the discussion often leaves MB struggling so what chance for those of us who lack a research team? Bill plugged away and Norbert searched the recesses of his memory for some coherent ideas. I think all this rather

detracted from their appreciation of Maiden Castle but it added to the
ragged tapestry of our week.

THE GIANT

Bill and I had plotted a further treat for Norbert. We waved Goethe a
fond farewell and set off for Cerne Abbas. We did not reveal to Norbert
Cerne's special claim to fame and left him to search the landscape for
the promised monument. I think he said: 'Good grief!' but it may have
been some private Germanic profanity. Discussion about the meaning
of the Giant does not require a kick-start from Melvyn Bragg. For a
long time it was assumed to be ancient. The latest notion, from recent
archaeology, suggests the figure was a late 17th Century lampoon
directed at the obsessions of the Puritan regime. A major part of the
mystery is that the first known written reference to the Giant is from
1764, almost a century later. Did no-one notice it being constructed
and record the happening?

If it is ancient surely someone from old Cerne, with a swan's quill and
some ink, must have thought it worth a mention in their jottings on a dull
winter's evening. And travellers must have noticed the village's outstanding
feature. Medieval monks may have chosen to allow the carving to grass
over to protect everyone from its explicit sexuality and aggression.
Victorian hypocrisy deleted the phallus from the carving. It conveys an
unambiguous message about fertility but also has the character of a
cartoon. Norbert observed that the Giant would be unremarkable to the
members of a down-to-earth mediaeval village community. It seems now
mainly to be a source of amusement and amazement. We were left with
just one further dilemma: to which of his many bishop-acquaintances
should Norbert send the picture postcard Bill had supplied?

BACK TO SCHOOL

We fell to talking of school and childhood. Bill went to a private day
school as an infant. As a result he was in a class just about half the size
of the one I joined on my fifth birthday. We each recall being taught

the basics of language and number effectively, mainly by rote. He had more opportunities for drama, music and sport but was troubled at the overt snobbery that justified his school's existence. One of my early heroes was 'Sam' Smallwood, who steered a lot of us through the eleven plus tests and, one afternoon a week, on his own, organised cane basketry successfully for a class of forty eight children. An exhibit survives in my garage.

Bill's memory is vivid about the extensive use of corporal punishment, more for the gratification of a few sadistic teachers than in the interests of maintaining order. This continued into his secondary school, a private day institution of high repute. The privilege of inflicting beatings was shared with prefects. It beggars belief that parents were paying good money to have their sons beaten for fun. No doubt it never did them any harm. Such happenings were rare in my primary school, but routine after that.

Norbert experienced a bizarre series of events in which a thoughtlessly violent teacher hit him hard and cut his face badly. The mother who had faced down an armed American GI was not to be fazed by an ill-tempered teacher and took the school to task. The teacher was duly removed. Some time later came a letter thanking her for stopping him relying on physical threat. It had rescued his career and he had become a better teacher. Casual violence was commonplace, for instance hurling a board rubber at boys in the back row and dropping of desk lids on fingers. We all three were conditioned to accept that our schools were entitled to behave much as they chose with very limited accountability; and we remain grateful to those caring and thoughtful teachers who shaped our aspirations positively despite the prevailing culture.

ON THE CLIFFS TO INDIA

The day ended with the slowest of strolls along the cliffs during which we turned the focus onto Norbert's personal and professional history, only fragments of which had surfaced in our shifting conversations. India played an important part in Norbert's life. There are twenty million Catholics in India. He went to Bombay in 1969 to take on responsibility for trainee priests. His first priority was to strip them of their vestments and send them out in local dress amongst the city's poorest to identify the most important needs for the Church to address. This galvanised the young priests but troubled the traditional authorities in both college and city. He also strove to establish a purposeful dialogue between Catholics and Hindus, an alliance that shaped much of the rest of his career.

Norbert was forced to leave after three years, a departure which caused serious dissent in the college community. He later returned to Benares Hindu University, then made his career in German Universities, specialising in dialogue between faiths. Many of the young men he trained in the early 1970s are now leaders of the Church in India and still close friends. Change for the Church has moved in parallel with political developments. As European authority has diminished, a more authentically rooted Indian church has emerged – a source of great satisfaction to Norbert.

Norbert has been involved in major inter-faith initiatives in various conflict zones, including Bosnia. European leaders are acutely aware that the ruinous path to conflict between the West and Islam, with its implications for terrorism, drug trafficking, civil unrest and de-stabilisation, is beyond military management. Dialogue between faiths, at all levels, has moved from the 'desirable' category into the 'essential' in reducing conflicts. Norbert is still in demand – I have wrestled with his diary – as one who understands how faiths can best find common ground. He has a vision as to how world faiths can make progress together without sacrificing the essence of their identity. The European Church has been slowest of all to grasp this; but a sense of urgency is emerging.

ON CHESIL BEACH

We set foot on Chesil Beach at its widest, just below the causeway to the Isle-with-no-name. The vast bank of pebbles noisily absorbed a strong sea swell. To the north the Beach curved away to infinity. We saw a satellite image of the IWNN later in the day; it hangs like a droplet from the silver thread of the Beach. The fossil-bearing strata in the cliffs at Charmouth belong to geological time; Chesil Beach is a relatively recent creation that even touches the span of early human history. It began to form ten thousand years ago, after the last Ice Age, as rivers of melted ice water dragged fragmented rock debris down to the still dry (English) Channel, adding it to previous deposits. The flood water generated rising sea levels and, eventually, as the Channel was opened to the Atlantic, huge waves drove water, rocks, and, in time, pebbles eastwards.

The massive limestone bulwark of Portland (sorry Bill) held up the bank of pebbles, which runs from Bridport to the island – some twenty eight kilometres; at its widest Chesil Beach is two hundred metres, and at its highest thirteen metres. The size of pebbles increases west to east. It is vulnerable in the most severe weather – even more so under the impact of climate change. So as the Beach was being battered into its final shape the first settlers were already laying claim to mainland Dorset. The lagoon behind the Beach was formed later as sea levels rose, creating a natural harbour – and an abundant resource for swans (and monks).

THE ISLE OF PORTLAND

Portland stands imposingly over the southern end of Chesil Beach. We confessed that we could understand Bill's reaction to its aspect. The scarp slope rises suddenly from a flat plain and the sea. It is covered with industrial, military and custodial buildings. The harbour was busy with commercial, naval and ferry vessels.

Fittingly but sadly this was Bill's moment to return home to family and his unpaid staff. So Norbert and I set off bravely to explore his dreaded Portland at first hand. Although it has no major settlement, Portland is quite heavily populated. Where the houses end the quarries, ancient and modern, begin. Processes are now highly mechanised and few people employed, but the wonderful deep-bedded limestone is still being worked. Residual materials are re-cycled for road aggregates. Portland stone has been used all over the world, most notably by Wren in St Paul's and other London churches, and for the Cenotaph in Whitehall. To the southern, lower, end of the

Portland stone – strong enough for bridges and churches, workable
enough for subtle sculpture

Portland Bill – winch for loading stone in foreground, coastal huts
behind, with Dorset cliffs beyond

island, on various headlands, stand platforms and winches that lifted the stone onto boats. The magic of the stone lies in its subtle pale colouring, its strength and durability and the ease with which it can be sculpted. There are some beautiful, intricate items carved from single pieces of rock at the little museum near Ope Cove.

We climbed the Portland Bill lighthouse, exactly a century old, to view the headland. The original light, built in 1788, is now a bird observatory. Portland Bill itself is an unusual place, a long way from the mainland, windswept and flat, dominated by the lighthouse and with a vast colony of beach huts. Single storey outbuildings have been converted for visitor services. We saw it in warm sun on a benign day. When the gales rage, it must be seriously bleak and an evil trap for ships over the centuries. The isle does more than its social duty in housing hundreds of prisoners and young offenders. It recently hosted a prison ship. The custodial buildings are not obtrusive but they add no comfort to the place. Its character is distinctive, rugged and independent, with a signature in stone across the world. It could be a thousand miles from lush, comfortable Dorset; and all the more worth visiting.

COASTAL GEMS

Norbert and I now headed for Durdle Door, yet another surprise for him but lacking the subtlety of Cerne Abbas. I feared that, in the decades since I was last here, the conjurors of tourist attractions might have given DD a gruesome makeover. Happily it is too difficult of access and too precious to be so mistreated. A huge car-park high on the cliffs there may be, but the walk out to the best ever sea arch remains a dramatic pleasure. I had not anticipated such perfect light to greet us but it was quite magical, with the slim silhouette of Portland on the skyline and the arch itself by turns green, black and golden as angles changed. The bays to the east wore an Aegean aspect with golden sand and arcs of green-blue sea. To the west a longer stretch of gravelly sand, raked with different colours and enclosed by a smaller arch, presented a rhythmic echo to Durdle Door itself. We clambered on to the narrow edge above the Arch and sat silently just gazing out

Durdle Dor arch looking across to silhouette of Isle of Portland

to sea. I feared another sect might arise from the inspiration of DD, but the Python muse was dormant. A place to linger.

My confidence was falsely raised by Durdle Door and I assured Norbert that Lulworth Cove had a beauty to match it. The Cove has evidently become the honeypot of all Dorset honeypots, with a massive carpark, redbrick tourist shops, and broad, stepped, tarmac paths to carry the legions up and down hills once made of grass. All of which overwhelms the cove, four fifths of a complete circle, and smaller than I remembered. We took seats by the shore outside a small café – which immediately closed for the day. The light was still marvellous and we would have sat longer but for the urgent, noisy stacking of chairs.

Time pressed anyway for us to move on to our accommodation near Corfe Castle. Purbeck wraps you immediately in its rich, sensuous colour and warmth. Just as when we had seen Stonehenge a few days earlier, we both gasped as the Castle itself came into view. Built to defend a gap between hills, it is concealed from several angles. The testament to its importance is evident in the exaggeratedly ruinous state of its buildings. Raggeh Omar has reported in front of structures more intact than this.

Our new residence was again of high standard, with some eccentric features. Why, in a huge bedroom, was the bathroom only slightly bigger than a telephone kiosk? The gold-painted chairs in the dance/function room also begged a few questions. Unreserved commendation must to be recorded for the New Inn at Church Knowle, an authentic four hundred year old building, with happy staff and an excellent local menu. If you want to see how a pub should look and be run, search no further. They even ensured a clear cold sky, full of rare stars, from a deeply dark village. Just one more treat: a small deer loping safely over the road on our return journey.

Our last day began in Corfe village in a rush hour to compete with many a town. It was disappointing to find that much of the castle was closed – not for safety reasons but as result of an unexplained 'conservation issue'. I now visited upon Norbert a mild tirade about the National Trust. What the NT has achieved for the protection of natural beauty on our coasts is priceless. As a custodian of buildings, it struggles to reconcile its priorities. Does it exist primarily to enable the great British (and German) public to enjoy important sites? Or to ensure the perfection of architectural features even if no-one gets to see them? History has been brutal to Corfe Castle. If it could fall down then please keep me out. But the conservators owe it to NT site managers and its public to explain openly the restrictions it imposes. English Heritage sites are open all year round; surely the NT could at least offer a few days each month for most properties during our cheerless winters? But thanks forever for protecting so much of the coastline.

We returned to the matchless coastal path that is the joy of south west England. Durlston was almost deserted, apart from a group of happy ramblers, kitted out for the Arctic. We walked along to the Dancing Ledge, with its quarrymen's pool, bitten at every step by the spiky wind but exhilarated by the chance to walk on wild cliffs above a troubled sea. We returned by a parallel path just 100m above. This was a foolhardy decision for which we both cheerfully denied responsibility. The wind gathered unreasonable strength as it hurtled up from the cliffs. Across the fields we saw the arctic ramblers again and envied them. I suggested to Norbert that they might be pursuing him as the sect guru, expecting him to share his humble cheese sandwich with all twenty of them. His response was not wholly worthy of a sect leader. We skulked behind low lines of bushes for protection from the wind, gradually tacking towards Durlston. Wind-tanned we may have been, but this is a magnificent walk in any weather.

I had just one more bright idea for the day, to which Norbert's good nature offered no resistance – Studland Beach. My mistake was to go to south rather than middle beach. I had forgotten that south beach is narrow and often over-populated with watersports enthusiasts – although today it was bleakly empty. The debris left by Bank Holiday visitors remained undisturbed by either the tide or beach cleaners, if such there be. The view to Old Harry Rocks was a wonder though.

An hotel above the beach provided – served would be an exaggeration – a tea bag in a cup of warm water, with UHT milk, on grim tables, and a carpet as neglected as the beach. No doubt it had been a busy weekend and today was sleepily quiet – but UHT milk in a county full of fine creamy cattle?

A final meal, and more outrageous ecclesiastical tales, at Church

Knowle, definitely the finest pub anywhere, concluded a fascinating week. It was good to reflect how these few days had set aside thirty seven years to renew, with much laughter and debate, more lost friendships.

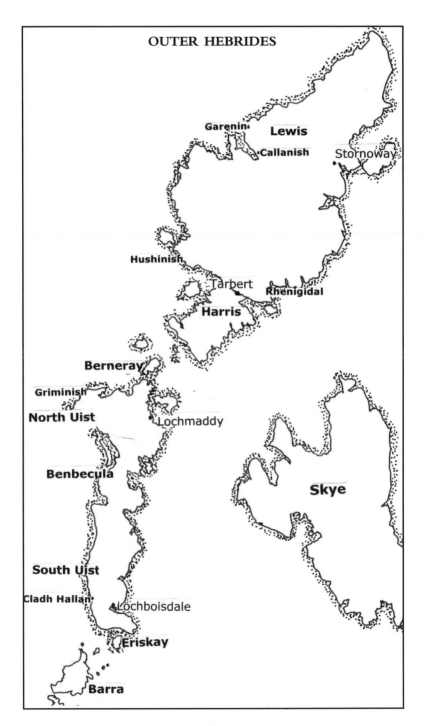

OUTER HEBRIDES

Garenin
Lewis
Callanish
Stornoway

Hushinish
Tarbert
Rhenigidal
Harris

Berneray
Griminish
North Uist
Lochmaddy

Benbecula

Skye

South Uist
Cladh Hallan
Lochboisdale

Eriskay

Barra

5.   ISLANDS AT THE EDGE OF THE SEA

THE IDEA OF VISITING the Outer Hebrides had long been a vague ambition for my son, Richard, and me. We are seasoned travellers together, accomplished in attracting hostile weather and familiar with the twin joys of highland Scotland – rain and midges. We have looked often enough at the maps, at pictures of beaches too good to be true, at blurred horizons to the far west, and at the lengthy, costly, ferry journeys. Now we set aside the excuses and rewarded Caledonian MacBrayne handsomely for a Hopscotch ticket to take us south to north through the islands. It is claimed that the trip out to the isles is relatively cheap, but after a week or so of being lashed by Atlantic gales soft incomers are prepared to pay a high premium to be returned to their nests. We paid no heed to such scurrilous nonsense.

The evocative translation of 'Hebrides' is 'islands at the edge of the sea'. Two hundred islands, of which just thirteen are inhabited, stretch over one hundred and forty tortuous kilometres. Along the western seaboard lie some of Europe's most stunning beaches, to the east a twisted, thin-soiled, gneiss coastline. To the far south the archipelago starts in a scattering of uninhabited rocky islets, then Barra, a small but thriving community. Next come the unusual almost sub-marine landscapes of the Uists. An angry blender of sea and rocks separates this from the lunar landscapes and grand mountains of Harris. Finally Lewis, misshapen, flat, laden with thousands of tons of peat, and exceptionally rich in pre-history. In previous millennia, in a more congenial climate, these islands supported a large, self-sufficient population; evidence can be found at every turn.

We knew that our few days could only give us mere impressions of this unique, complex landscape and its communities past and present; but at last we were making a start. Both of us relish remoteness but we sensed that the Western Isles, the last inhabited outpost of Britain, might still be disconcerting.

The seven hour ferry journey from Oban, even on a dull day, is compelling on all sides, through Mull Sound, past Morvern and Ardnamurchan, the ghosts of Coll, Tiree, Rum, Eigg and Muck, and soon the silhouettes of Barra and the Uists ahead. The Minch was eerily calm for us. In a way it was disappointing, at least for me, not to experience it in a more savage mood. Richard was quietly contented. He had, I discovered later, endured an hour of spectacular sea-sickness on the Stranraer ferry a couple of years before. The light started to fail as we left Castlebay, on Barra, for the final hour to Lochboisdale, during which rain began to spear down. The Hebrides' weather arrives predominantly from the west but, during our trip, winds swept in from all points of the compass. On a darkening Sunday night Lochboisdale recalled images of Port Stanley. The minimal harbour loomed eerily out of the gloaming as the ferry master deftly navigated a treacherous channel and, like a nautical boy-racer, performed a perfect handbrake turn into the dock. We winced and stifled our shouts of advice about the unforgiving rocks slicing inches past the ship.

THE FAR SOUTH

The settlement of Lochboisdale is low lying and scattered randomly on hummocks of grass and rock which decline into the sea without much sign of a struggle. The route to our accommodation wove circuitously along a ribbon of tarmac. The dim light did not flatter the pebble-dashed houses; nor did the items of apparently derelict agricultural machinery outside every second dwelling. Richard took to his bed perversely satisfied with the aura of bleakness, augmented by a grim weather warning issued by an apologetic guesthouse proprietor. If you spend seven hours on a ferry you are entitled to a memorable experience at the end of it; the Uists, we felt, would not let us down.

We took breakfast alongside other guests who were a little too keen to tell us how wonderful the weather had been for the last ten days. Well, we thought, they can keep their bright, soft sunshine; we have come to experience the real Hebrides. So we ventured out from the cocoon of the guesthouse into the teeth of a gale (a gentle breeze to locals). Our impressions of the little town were favourably modified in the morning light, abetted by welcoming conversations with the guest house owner and with staff in an excellent tourist office. The Gaelic accent is so engaging that even bad news about incoming weather sounds quite the best prospect you could imagine. They fell however into the dreaded 'if only you'd been here last week' mantra which is hard to forgive. We were met everywhere with natural warmth, unfailing courtesy and a quiet willingness to talk.

It took a while, as on Orkney, to adjust to a treeless landscape. The hinterland of Lochboisdale is well populated with a scattering of modern housing and an air of modest prosperity. The primary school looked encouragingly busy, its car park overflowing. The primacy of Gaelic is evidenced in road signs and public notices, all with smaller, eye-straining English translations. We were quickly disabused of our assumption, from the guidebooks, that South Uist is emphatically Catholic and the rest of islands wholly Protestant. Richard claimed to have been looking forward to a north-south border marshalled by buckle-shoed Puritans, ready to wield a stick at anyone over-exerting themselves on the Sabbath. Folk still hold to their religions, but those we met wore their allegiances lightly. South Uist now has its Kirk, and its Wee Free congregation, to complement the many Catholic roadside shrines, statues and monuments. Churches of all kinds abound.

Other signs of change also dawned on us quickly during that first morning. Crofting has, of course, become only an exceptional way of life. Farming now means tending livestock dispersed widely over the hillsides. There is little of the lushness of Orkney. Rearing sheep and cattle looks like a tough business. Fishing is in evidence only on a small scale, and apart from high quality smoked salmon, the menus reflect this. From the guest house and the supermarket, we concluded that most food is now imported by ferry.

Our overall plan required us to strike north but we felt impelled first to turn south to Eriskay, forever famous as the island whose dubious good fortune inspired the book, and film, Whisky Galore. We trundled over the long causeway – a product largely of EU funding. Perhaps a pattern was already beginning to emerge. The relative independence of these islands is, it seems, being reduced by a combination of factors: the frequent, subsidised roll-on roll-off ferries, rarely halted by bad weather, increasing air links, new inter-island causeways and incoming investment derived from EU priority status, in collaboration with the Highlands and Islands Development Board (HIDB).

Everywhere there are the signs of a growing tourist infrastructure but the number of visitors reaches capacity for only a few weeks in summer. The remoteness of the islands will always inhibit large scale tourism outside that peak season. We began to wonder whether the fabric of a genuinely local economy can ever be robust enough to sustain these communities long term. In a different era, over-dependence on the mainland dragged the St Kilda community to its sad end. These islands have many more options to sustain their own identity, but there is justifiable unease at the web they have entered.

ERISKAY

Once across the causeway we headed for the 'SS Politician' public house. As boring near-teetotallers, we had little interest in contraband hooch but we were deceived by legend into expecting a low-pitched traditional, thatched, inn that would enliven the story of the cargo ship which foundered nearby in 1941. Although it records those events well enough, the small pub is just a humble modern bungalow with a Tennants' sign swinging forlornly in the wind. Nearby a pair of teenagers emerged from the local school and hopped over the fence. We tried to imagine what terrors or tedium could have been occurring inside the school to make a windswept, sodden bus shelter a more powerful attraction. Richard observed that it was probably a history lesson.

Close to the Eriskay ferry terminal is the beach where Bonnie Prince Charlie first landed on the Uists in July 1745. Romantic legend apart, there seems little to celebrate about the arrival of this unlikely hero. A fine talisman he may have been, but lacking military nous, the raw courage and even the language of his hardy native followers. The story of his arrival set the tone. Apparently he insulted his rescuers on the beach, spurned their fish at table and baulked at sleeping on a traditional seaweed bed. If it had not been for the indisputable heroine of the piece, Flora McDonald, whose birthplace is a popular tourist attraction, he might well have remained on the island in foppish despair.

The beach itself is strikingly beautiful. The sand and water here have a luminous quality that produces an irridescent gold and blue light even without sunshine. Richard was sufficiently tempted to go paddling so as to re-enact the arrival of his flawed hero, but came out when he could no longer feel his feet. So much for the Gulf Stream.

CLADH HALLAN

In search for some more robust links to the distant past, we headed to our first encounter with the prolific ancient history of the Hebrides. The new museum at Kildonan impressed us because, as well as

A stately heron – conserving his energy while waiting for fish to come to him

76

displaying a coherent view of the past, it also connects admirably with recent archaeological research. If archaeological finds had a commercial value, like peat or wind energy, then the Hebrides would be rejoicing in a flood of wealth and celebrity. Various universities are involved on different sites across the islands. As the emergent University of the Highlands establishes itself, no doubt the volume of activity will increase. In the next decade we should see more coherent interpretations emerging of the peoples that first occupied the islands.

Our immediate interest was drawn to Daliburgh on the west coast north from Lochboisdale. Excavations here in the last few years have exposed three stone double roundhouses at Cladh Hallan, dated at 1000BC. Immediately adjacent are four more, as yet unexcavated. So this was a communal village, constructed into the ground with solid floors and built up with timber, turf and reeds. It is not as spectacular as Skara Brae but there are obvious similarities, not least in the location by the western dunes. Over two hundred other pre-historic sites have been identified on the west side of the Uists alone.

Cladh Hallan itself has much else to reveal. Only ten per cent of the potential settlement area across the fertile machair has been excavated. The rest may well be the abandoned sites of other generations. Immediately we started to register that the pre-historic population of the islands must have been quite dense, perhaps like Orkney, even Salisbury Plain or Dorset.

Beneath the house sites the archeologists found mummified (deliberately preserved) bodies, male, female, young, adult and old. Forensic analysis affirms that these bodies were retained (tanning in peat) for several hundred years before being buried beneath the dwellings, presumably in veneration of ancestors. Alternatively these particular buildings may have been a ritual 'house of the dead', never occupied by the living. Such practices are found in contemporary societies in South America. To 21st Century minds, distracted from the spirituality that has always been fundamental to human existence, this may seem macabre and gruesome. Sad to record, the excavated houses at Cladh Hallan have started to fill with water and to collect other debris (including an unaccountable number of shoes) possibly from winter storms, possibly from gormless beach trippers. The latter should beware of digging too vigorously to make their sandcastles; nasty shocks from the deep past could await them.

As we explored the ancient village and burial sites, we caught sight of a funeral service, with perhaps three hundred mourners, in the Catholic cemetery on top of the cliffs. The soils in many parts of the Hebrides are very thin; over the centuries those seeking to dig for foundations or to bury their dead have been drawn to the same stretches of the western coastline, carrying bodies for many miles across mountain and moorland. Maybe in earliest times there was some symbolism in burying the dead close to the sea facing west.

We ventured onto the huge beach beyond Cladh Hallan. By Hebridean standards it is impressive more in scale than beauty, with a slight tang of rotting seaweed, or worse, in the air. I indulged my modest artistic bent by taking photographs of some unusual windblown sand formations, while Richard threw rocks at them. As if in anger at the rock hurling or even the illicit photography, the sky grew suddenly dark and heavy, spiky rain cut into us as we fled.

We retreated to the splendid café at the museum. On the wall were photographs of food being delivered to St Kilda in harsh times, a sobering image to accompany our lunch snacks. I decided to take my note pad to the table to make some jottings on our journey so far. Unfortunately the very hospitable café manager may have assumed I was writing a report on the food, or even the dreaded health and safety compliance. I was given extra oatcakes; but next time I will write out in the rain.

TESTING WATERS

In a strengthening, wet north-easterly wind, our thoughts turned to our accommodation for the night. We were interested in the numerous small hostels in the islands, described in guidebooks with ominously indeterminate phrases such as 'fairly basic', 'ungraded' and 'recently renovated'. Our first port of call met all three of those descriptors. Everywhere seemed slightly damp, beneath a suspect thatched roof, with elderly bunks and bedding. Both of us feigned bravado initially, admiring the 'character' of the place, but privately hoping the other would crack. So we agreed to blame each other for the decision to move on, with our tougher-than-Bonnie-Prince-Charlie credentials in tatters. On a warm sunny day we would definitely have stayed there. Honest.

We also realised, rather belatedly, that these islands are quite big and the roads slow. We really needed to be further north. The guidebooks and maps had partly prepared us for the next part of our journey, across Benbecula, but the reality, in driving rain, was still quite disturbing. The bleak flatness and endless rocky-rimmed craters of dark water create an impression of being chest deep in the incoming sea. The causeways are in many places reassuringly lined by huge square boulders. Just how horrendous the conditions were when five lives were lost in a car on such a causeway a couple of winters ago is unimaginable. A high tide, severe westerly winds and appalling visibility must have contributed, but the idea that a loaded vehicle could be lifted from the causeway and tipped into the sea beyond is just too terrifying to contemplate. Wise old heads on the islands apparently raised concerns about the building of so many causeways, each of which stands as an obstruction to previously natural routes for tides and storms. The elements will never loosen their grip out here.

LOCHMADDY

We headed north east for Lochmaddy, the only town on North Uist, along a road undergoing conversion from single to double track. Large numbers of JCBs, diggers and dumpers were clawing their ugly way through miles of sodden peat moorland. A mere car had no place in this giant's playground and we were relieved to reach the small Outdoor Centre in Lochmaddy, which had hostel accommodation to serve our purposes well enough. It also had a stock of canoes for emergency escapes if, as seemed increasingly likely, the need arose. Our evening respite from the relentless rain was a meal in the Scandinavian style, red clapperboard, hotel which has enhanced the town's image in the business and tourist stakes. I have to admit that I did briefly consider whether to abandon Richard to the hostel and book in to this warm, welcoming 4 star hotel instead. Would my conscience have let me sleep? Quite possibly.

TRAVELLERS' TALES

Richard and I have found common cause in modestly adventurous travels for twenty years, although inevitably our interests have diverged. In the early days, when I carried the rucsac and paced myself so that he could keep up, we shared the delights of the Yorkshire Dales and began some forays into the mountains. In more equal times we camped by little lakes in Snowdonia and set off on an episodic venture along the wonderful South-West coast path, the last ninety kilometres of which remain to be tackled. By stages Richard has become more of a mountaineer than I ever was and his level of fitness has risen as mine has slowed down. It is good to have someone carrying your gear – just so long as you can catch up with them when you need a drink.

The natural tensions in our travelling relationship arise from Richard's enthusiasm to tackle hard routes at speed as against my inclination for frequent pauses to play with cameras and binoculars. For him the spiny ridge is instinctively more interesting than the prospect of a soaring eagle or a moving shaft of sunlight. However we are accomplished at generous compromise and improvisation. He compensates for a venture-too-gentle by disappearing on a strenuous run as soon as we arrive at our destination. Our travels seem to fall into a fairly natural balance between intensive discussions, observational humour, brain games and easy silences while we just absorb our surroundings. I remain convinced that on the coastal path Richard would contrive to pose me some irresistibly interesting question about the meaning of life or the plight of the Palestinians, just as we were about to strike up the steepest slopes. He tried later to persuade me that he wrote significant parts of his A level General Studies from these discussions. We still talk endlessly, but I now learn more from him than vice versa.

THE ELUSIVE CORNCRAKE

Next morning I tested the limits of these natural tensions by heading for the RSPB base at Balranald on the north-west extremity of the Uists. A group of birdwatchers had already set off

**The elusive corncrake seeking the limelight at Balranald
RSPB Centre**

on a walk with the warden so we contented ourselves with a brief
look around the tiny centre. Through the window I heard a
repetitive rasping sound which I took to be either a recording or a
decoy. The surprising reality was that a corncrake was prowling the
long grass in the small RSPB compound. The corncrake is not the
most exciting of birds, either by its appearance or behaviours; but its
claim to fame is that is very secretive and difficult to locate. It is not
supposed to strut by on an open stage, like a dog at Crufts, just a few
feet from onlookers. Could this one have been a rescue chick,
enjoying domestic adoption by the RSPB? Corncrakes are
notoriously bad neighbours for humans. Their call, a single tone,
rasping rattle, is distinctive and harsh. It also goes on for hour after
hour from dawn. For passers-by, it was nonetheless a fortunate
discovery. Richard was unimpressed. Why is there so much interest
in a drab, unadventurous, inedible bird with an ugly, relentless call?
Sorry RSPB.

A HAUNTING HORIZON

Indisputably exciting for both of us was the horizon that greeted us soon after we left Balranald for Griminish Point. The unmistakable and unexpected profile of St Kilda, at least forty miles away, rose grey and abrupt from an otherwise endless ocean. The massive bird-laden cliffs, the last nail of the old world, witnessed a gradual but inexorable decline in a community that finally gave up the ghost in 1932. A lure to adventurous spirits ever since, these small islands have a melancholy history. Several books tell the story sympathetically and graphically. It is difficult to imagine that the harsh characteristics of the St Kilda environment are replicated anywhere else in the Northern Hemisphere. Its remoteness, exaggerated by the wildest of seas, did not deter ancient settlers and later – notably Norse – invaders. The Vikings were feeling their way westwards, step by precarious step, along the northern shores of the Atlantic. Remoteness and high seas were of little concern to such hardened adventurers.

The final years of the St Kilda community deserve attention. It is beyond my comprehension that they survived so long on the islands.

St Kilda's lofty cliffs on the horizon 40 miles distant

The population was never more than one hundred throughout the final century of the settlement, falling eventually to just thirty six. Life depended on the ghastly, perilous harvesting of gannets and fulmars for fuel and food, with fish, mutton, milk and potatoes as supplements. Exposed to increasing numbers of visitors from 1750 onwards, the community succumbed to a dreadful array of infectious diseases. Worst of all was the 'Eight day sickness' – tetanus – which by the 1860s was claiming the lives of over six in ten newborn infants. One day in five produces gale force winds. There must have been a powerful pride and sense of identity to sustain the St Kilda generations through such insupportable grief and toil. Whatever the privations over time of the rest of the Outer Hebrides, these can hardly compare to the prolonged torments of the St Kildan village.

We walked separately and slowly across the Griminish peninsular, each contemplating that distant horizon and the story it conjured. The sun now surreptitiously made its first serious appearance of our journey and the stunning beauty of the headland, the coast and the islands came to life. The moment remains vivid.

When we returned to our vehicle, parked at the end of a rough

Richard on Griminish in contemplative mood looking out towards ghostly St Kilda

track near an apparently abandoned house, we were greeted by its sole resident, a man of ninety seven. This has been his home for seventy years, his nearest neighbour two kilometres away. Now on his own, frail, with poor sight and mobility he showed great spirit and seemed to enjoy his chat with two strangers from the far, far south. We wondered how his life is sustained on lonely Griminish. I will picture him again when the grip of dark winter and severe storms return.

BIG ISSUES

Our encounter with this spirited old man triggered a conversation for us that lasted intermittently until we returned home. There are few subjects that Richard and I have left untouched in our exchanges while walking over the years, whether politics, beliefs, education, histories, sport, music, life choices or just the people, places and happenings we come across. So we know each other's views well enough. We had rehearsed before the ideas of the 'most favoured generation'. What would he now add to the balance sheet? What troubled him most?

His increasing concern is that we have not begun even to slow down the headlong exploitation of our planet's resources. Meanwhile global population grows exponentially. Even now, when the writing is on every available wall about climate change, democratic governments invest in high technology, high risk solutions rather than genuine sustainability. Underlying this is a refusal even to contemplate viable alternatives to endless economic growth which, on a finite planet with a growing population, is self evidently daft.

Richard identified another aspect of the same failure to face reality. More than Germany and France, we have progressively given up the ghost as manufacturing nation. We have allowed ourselves to waste our coal reserves, abandon our capacity to produce steel, ships, vehicles, and most consumer goods. We have failed to capitalise on our advantages in renewable energy. Had Germany been blessed with our constant tides and waves it would surely by now have harnessed power enough for the indefinite future. Progress is still possible but it is terrifyingly late in the day.

THE SOUNDS OF HARRIS

With such thoughts rattling us, we took the ferry across the Sound of Harris. I imagine that wise locals scoffed at the idea of a year-round ferry from Berneray to Leverburgh – a mere ten kilometres to map-fixated southern landlubbers. It is a perilous journey, perhaps twice as far, requiring accomplished seamanship. The vessel heads west through a slalom of buoys, between a torrent of rocky outcrops, turning

Mountain plateau on Harris, an austere, hostile environment

eventually north east until it slows to a hushed tiptoe through scarily shallow waters. I wanted to lead a round of applause for the skipper, but no-one could wrest their clenched fingers from the ship's rails. Put him in charge of national policy on renewable tidal energy.

The Isle of Harris is shaped like a strangled figure of eight – South Harris nearly circular, North Harris wrapped tightly around a wild mountain range, bordering onto low-lying Lewis. South Harris itself is magnificently varied and beautiful, very wild and daunting. We took the sinuous route on the west of the island towards Tarbert. The scenery is too distracting for safe driving. We stuttered along the coast stopping at every turn to gasp at the luminescent golden beaches whose brilliance defied an overcast sky. Tottering down the rocks to explore this elemental phenomenon, we were assaulted by lashing, horizontal rain while the beach still shone at our feet. Across the water lay gloomy Taransay, the castaway island of the BBC series in 2000, decidedly uninviting.

The delights of the coast turn east into the badlands of wild and rocky terrain over to Tarbert. An award must go to the engineers who designed the improbable route across this endless lofty tumble of gneiss, heather and a few spoonfuls of soil, a really menacing environment. And so to Tarbert, tightly packed by mountains north and south, and harbours, east and west, into the pivot of the Harris figure-of-eight. We enjoyed our first wander through the little town, solid and attractive, with more shops and services than we expected.

Once again we played with a decision about where to spend the night. Our imaginations had been fired already by the description of the youth hostel at Rhenigidal, a further twenty twisting kilometres along the east coast. Had we come all this way to stay only in the towns? The shops were closing and we had no food. It was stick or twist. We chose delay by eating fish and chips in the evening sun. The fish vendor contributed brutally to the debate about Rhenigidal. In a deft blend of Gaelic and Anglo-Saxon he advised that it was a ★★★★★★★ long way and there was ★★★★ ★★★ to see or do when you arrived. Anyway this was the challenge we needed. The poet laureate of Tarbert had spoken. We took the steep, tortuous road to Rhenigidal.

The evening sun completed the anticipated delight of this hamlet, pitched at the end of a Hebridean fjord. By name, location, and

**Rhenigidal youth hostel perfectly located at
the end of the world on Harris**

scattered settlement pattern, this was an authentic Norse community, with a spectacular, moody harbour, calm and turbulent by turns. Rhenigidal can genuinely lay claim to being 'the remotest hostel, in the deepest valley in the whole of Merrie Scotland'. The hostel, a traditional two storey, whitewashed, dwelling perches on a small ledge above a steep slope from the little road at the very end of the dale. The little house can, allegedly, sleep seventeen. We were just four the first night, and six the second, when it felt quite crowded. It had a magical quality and the memory stays with me.

One jarring note. Why, on an island laden with peat, scoured by massive winds, waves and tides, does this hostel burn coal (probably imported from Poland or South America) as its main source of heating?

Two German students, aged nineteen and twenty four, were already cooking tea when we arrived. Both spoke shamingly good English and had interesting stories to tell. The younger, with no experience of serious walking, or of the UK, had completed his social service year prior to university as a hospital volunteer. His inspiration came from a book of photographs of wonderful, blue-skied Scotland. He had worked extra hours to kit himself out with all the latest gear and walked the West Highland Way from Glasgow to Fort William in double quick time. So he continued across to Skye and thence to Harris, the end of his mission, having seen Scotland in all its moods. His compatriot, a scientist turned merchant banker, had spent a lot of time in the UK but had never experienced the delights of the highlands and islands. These were admirable ambassadors for their country and their generation – modest, articulate, enthusiastic, purposeful and humorous. Richard took off on a run up the horribly steep hillside, which made all of us feel tired. Later we four launched into one of those lengthy, meandering, lively late-night exchanges for which youth hostels were created.

INNER HARRIS

It was good to wake up in Rhenigidal, even on a rather dull and cloudy morning. We bade the two Germans farewell (one weakened sufficiently to accept a lift to the main road) and set off along the tiny coastal road towards Hushinish. Our objective was the remote mountain pass to Ullaval, to see the resident eagles and some extraordinary overhanging cliffs. Although the cloud level rose and fell before us as we walked, the necessary thermals never set in and the eagles sat out another hungry morning. We were mocked by a cuckoo, perfectly camouflaged against the rocks across the valley, announcing its successful adoption of some hapless little birds. The walk took us alongside the HEP pipeline which provides Harris with much of its electricity. On a distinct but tiny path we wound our way past some small lakes and up to a rocky pass. I took time out to watch in vain for my eagles through the gathering dark clouds. Richard pounded further into the next valley to survey the great overhang for climbing options.

Back at the road we chose to challenge the weather by driving on to Hushinish Bay at the end of the peninsula. The first joy was to drive within inches of the famous front door of Amhuinnsuidhe Castle, admiring the improbable achievements of the gardeners, and a glimpse ahead of that mystical golden disc in the sky. Hushinish came as another magnificent surprise, a massive, beautifully golden, gently curving beach, defined by green, rocky headlands. The views to the southern islands were superb but the wintry winds from the sea curtailed our sunbathing session – an exhilarating end to the afternoon.

A LITTLE STORM

Our second night at Rhenigidal was shared with two couples of my age. The Scottish couple were in pursuit of the last Corbetts (mountains over seven hundred and sixty metres) for their collection and had just claimed Clisham in the half-light. The others, from St Albans, were completing their coverage of Western Scotland, camping or hostelling all the way. Although Richard was now the only resident who could by any definition be considered a youth, the hostel company was congenial both for lively conversation and for managing a small space considerately. Many small and unfashionable English hostels are being sacrificed to market realities. The Scottish revival relies on cutting the costs – with a warden nearby only on a retainer, not a salary – and maximising the space available. In Rhenigidal the door is left unlocked and visitors trusted to pay their dues and treat the place well. In civilisation, further south, such assumptions may not apply. In the Hebrides anyway, the original vision of the hostel movement can still be made to work.

Seriously bad weather was forecast for the night and we noted the barometer falling through the evening. In the car, Richard and I listened to the final stages of Arsenal's defeat by Barcelona in the Paris final. I felt for Andrew and Peter (Bill of Dorset's boys) who will have been bitterly disappointed. And then came the rain. Storm force winds from the south battered Rhenigidal, with massive waves pounding the shore and wild spirals of water swirling across the headland. The hostel building was equal to it all, and worse no doubt. It was an exciting scene, a battle of the elements we rarely experience further south but commonplace hereabouts. For all our well waterproofed gear and experience of mountain weather, we moved off in the morning with some apprehension. Such days give you little rest, with the relentless noise and intrusion of wind and rain; yet this is routine for the locals who go about their business without a flicker of concern.

We made first for Stornoway along a well engineered, full sized road through some uninspiring territory comprising huge, bleak peat bogs and rocky outcrops. However, beauty is not all. The peat, laid down from about four thousand years ago, is estimated at a total of eighty five million tons. Each household is reckoned to use about fifteen thousand blocks a year, involving about fifteen man-days to cut and stack. Peat continues to grow in thickness year on year as the cold, wet and acidic conditions delay the decomposition of plants. So, it is claimed, this is a renewable source of heat, with more carbon dioxide being absorbed than burnt.

A fierce debate is now raging on Lewis over proposals to construct an industrial-scale wind turbine plant across hundreds of acres of its peat moorland. Much of the power generated would be exported to the mainland. The lure of large scale inward investment will be difficult to resist, but at the price of ruining its timeless landscape. The local mood is strongly hostile, according to media reports. Edinburgh will choose wind power before nuclear and the battalions are lining up for a long campaign. This exemplifies the dilemma of these islands as they struggle to offer their young people a prosperous future.

Stornoway is more convincingly a town than Tarbert, with suburbs, a sizeable supermarket, a modern hospital, and a windswept shopping precinct. After just a few days in the wilds we experienced some culture shock in approaching this scale of civilisation. We tried to imagine the town on a Sunday, with commerce and leisure sternly closed, and huge, dark-suited congregations —of up to fifteen hundred— attending lengthy church services. There are ten places of worship in the small central triangle of the town. So it is a place apart, immovably convinced of the decadence of the world across the water; and proof that traditional beliefs can be upheld against a very high tide, given enough energy and determination. We may feel uneasy at the intensity of Sabbath observance here, but no-rules Sundays elsewhere in the UK often seem rather dysfunctional and joyless. The Hebrides asserts its right to be different.

WEST SIDE STORIES

Stornoway was but a stepping stone for us on an historical trail along the west coast of Lewis. The prime feature of the Arnol Blackhouse Museum is a restored traditional Hebridean house, still occupied in the nineteen sixties. Dwellings like this have provided shelter for Hebrideans for centuries. The walls are of stone, a few feet thick, deeply founded in the soil, with stone slab floors and a thick, low-cast thatch roof, weighted down with large rock anchors on heavy ropes. As a response of humankind to a hostile environment, such house design, by its durability, is proof of great ingenuity and traditional skills. The crucial need was to create an indoor environment thoroughly proofed against the external elements. These houses combined living quarters for both humans and their animals. With the land of the croft, the traditional smallholding of the highlands, a harsh livelihood could, with good fortune, be sustained. There had to be land enough for a few animals and crops, and nearby fresh and sea waters for fish.

To 21st Century eyes and expectations, such living conditions are very harsh. In the reconstruction there are small windows but no chimney. The traditional logic was that the peat fire in the centre of the living room floor, which never goes out, generated a sooty deposit on to the thatch. This could be scraped and returned to the soil as a fertiliser. A few minutes of peat smoke was more than enough for our feeble lungs; what did it do for generations of blackhouse dwellers? The small box beds – wooden partitions – provided snug protection from the cold and damp; presumably it was warmer to sleep curled up rather than stretched out. How did their spines cope with such confinement though?

It does not take much imagination to backtrack from here to the

Blackhouse interior and the perpetual peat fire

double round houses at Cladh Hallan, to conjure up a way of life very similar to that at Arnol, continuing into the mid-twentieth century. The technologies are little changed. The essential contract for survival between the settler and the elements is the same. Richard can easily weary of historical exhibits – the poor lad was taken to too many as a child I fear – but he was mightily impressed by the Arnol Blackhouse.

A small visitor centre stands just thirty underwater steps along the lane from the Blackhouse. I took the chance of a conversation with the manager. Her readiness to talk led me to ask her whether she saw herself as Hebridean, Scottish, British or what. Her answer was emphatic – and she was confident many others in the community would agree: first of all she was Hebridean, then European. Initially we were surprised, but the response echoed what we had already seen for ourselves. Most developments that are making life on the islands acceptable in the new century, and enabling younger people to come back, have been funded by the EU, with the HIDB, through a strategic commitment to help integrate remote communities. EU funding has been forthcoming for causeways, road improvements, air and ferry links, cultural, sporting and tourist facilities. The Scottish Executive has joined in the investments.

The message, though, is clear: for decades governments in London and Edinburgh failed to make the Western Isles a sufficient priority. The EU has stolen a march on domestic government and is winning the loyalty of people at the roots of life on the islands.

The next port of call was Garenin, a splendidly restored village comprising several blackhouses, including another of the Gatliff small hostels. I suppose it was inevitable that the place looked rather like a film set (which it no doubt will be when the opportunity presents itself). The wind and rain were still close to storm pitch and we opted for just the briefest look around, before retreating to the (blackhouse) café. This however was full of Canadians, researching their roots in settlements dislocated by the 19th Century clearances and famines. This type of historical tourist attraction represents a sound investment in the Hebrides. If some good can be made now of the miseries of the clearances, then all strength to their elbows. Unfortunately two coachloads was too much for the small café; a battle of ancient scale and brutality was about to begin over the last few slices of quiche. We

Garenin village, a cluster of reconstructed Blackhouses on cliffs above the Atlantic

were now unused to such crowds, and in the spirit of the Bonnie Prince, we retreated and made our way to Callanish.

CALLANISH

Callanish, the most spectacular evidence of Neolithic culture in these islands, poses many questions. We were impressed with the new, high quality visitor centre. No excuse now, we thought, for failing to understand what this place was really about. But the more you learn here, the harder you look, the more complex the enigma becomes.

The central site, dating back four thousand years, is a stone circle with a lengthy avenue aligned just to the east of north and single lines of stones at the three other compass points. It was built on land that had long been cultivated and then left to pasture. Its imposing appearance speaks of power – but only for an interlude. The surrounding area has a host of other ritual sites, many still awaiting excavation.

A burial chamber at the heart of the central circle post-dates the

Callanish – mysterious Neolithic stone circles and avenues, probably tracing complex astronomical patterns

stones themselves. Much re-building and re-alignment have altered the site over time. It became dilapidated in the (increasingly wetter) centuries up to 1000BC; indeed it was probably despoiled, perhaps in a kind of ritual cleansing to create distance from the creed and people it once commemorated. By about 800BC it was abandoned and started to disappear under an accumulating peat blanket.

The orientation of the circle remains puzzling. Ingenious research suggests that on an eighteen and a half year pattern, the moon, viewed from the avenue, skims the hills of the southern horizon, like a god dancing a visit on the populace. Stone markers traced each point of lunar descent. I did not immediately take to this notion but am increasingly persuaded by it. The heavens are more visible and compelling to a community without artificial forms of light. The appeal of astronomy as the controlling force in the Neolithic world makes sense. It displaces the intensive affiliation of the living with their ancestors as a means of influencing the elements. We can imagine the political and religious power of astronomer-priests, but we have precious little evidence to play with.

The astonishing phenomenon which Callanish exemplifies is that within the space of just a few centuries (as defined now by hard scientific data), circles in wood, then in stone, orientated to solar or lunar phases, were being created across the islands we now call Britain and Ireland. Some still dominate their landscapes today. Thousands of others are smaller and easily overlooked despite assiduous mapping by the Ordnance Survey. The spreading creeds that justified this incredible investment of time and labour remain elusive. If we risk translating observations of isolated 19th and 20th Century low technology societies elsewhere, then belief in the continuing life of the spirits of people, animals, even plants, may be part of the explanation. Most sites show signs of ritual sacrifice. At Callanish traces of henbane and fungi might be evidence of hallucinatory happenings. The reasons for the abandonment of these places and their re-use for agriculture or dwellings (as at Callanish) in subsequent millennia are also beyond us; except that societies rarely stand still. Somehow whenever we touch the enigmatic creativity of places such as Callanish, an electric pulse stirs our curiosity anew.

As we peeled away from Callanish we pored intensively over what we had just seen. It is an inspirational place and an extraordinary achievement. We reflected that the site speaks of terrible fears, borne no doubt from the fragility and harshness of life at the time. It is difficult to think of any parallels from the last thousand years to compare with the scale of such massive stone enterprises. The great medieval castles and cathedrals were expressions of power in prosperous, well established societies with relatively advanced technologies. The temples of the industrial revolution express the confidence and ambition of that age. The burial chambers and great cairns arise amidst village farming communities on the brink of survival. Some researchers into the stone circles detect signs that these societies were expanding and becoming more stratified, with wealth and power being concentrated within a few families. Maybe the emblems of astronomy served a political purpose as well.

Richard then observed that even these most eloquent expressions of humankind's fears, beliefs, and inspirations are utterly tiny when viewed against the elemental powers all around them. Above all the vast dark night skies must have been overwhelming, especially in the depths of winter. Our floodlit world obscures our appreciation of this. We tend to be more aware of the mountains, the seas, the storms, the rivers than the skies. We cannot hope to appreciate the mindset of the Ancients when they set their best before the deities of their age. Perhaps like the greatest ever scientific minds such as da Vinci, Newton and Darwin, they viewed their achievements from a humble perspective, just playing with pebbles on a beach while they searched for meaning in the universe. We had returned to some simple truths through our journey to the outer edges of the outer isles.

A GOLDEN ROAD

We sped back to Tarbert for a short night prior to joining the 07.30 ferry to Skye. A motel fifty metres from the ferry dock met our needs –functional and minimalist (apart from the price) as it was. Richard settled in to the nine square metre twin room while I started to sort our gear. Our first TV of the week, to Richard's delight, featured one Spongebob Squarepants, a cartoon character I had not previously encountered. From Callanish to Squarepants in an hour. Richard redeemed his reputation later by discovering an illuminating documentary made for local TV about the Flannan Isles, a true story immortalised in the poem by Wilfred Wilson Gibson about the mysterious disappearance of three lighthouse keepers.

Our last project for this visit to Harris was the Golden Road which clings to the east coast of the south island. The melancholy story echoes so many from mainland Scotland and the islands. For millennia the settlements of Hebrideans were on the western seaboard, where the machair provided a depth of soil for pasture and crops, and where building materials lay to hand. The endless shower of fragmented sea shells, swept by the winds, served as liming fertiliser for the land. Survival on crofts had always been marginal but from about 1750 to 1820 the harvesting of kelp (seaweed ash), used in the production of glass and soap, provided a degree of meagre security for tenants and infamous prosperity for landlords. Kelp is the floating forest anchored in shallow waters off these shores. After the Napoleonic Wars new sources of kelp and more advanced industrial processes led to a rapid decline for the Hebridean trade.

Landowners (mainly resident in London and Edinburgh) followed the economic line of least resistance, letting their estates for sheep rearing and clearing the crofters to the eastern seaboard. Thousands of families escaped to Canada and elsewhere. Those who chose to remain had to come to terms with the more sheltered but rocky, almost soil-less, and gnarled east coast. This land was of little economic value and so was readily available. Even with the use of the inappropriately named 'Lazy Beds', low walled patches into which soil and sea weed were concentrated with ridges for planting, life was harsh beyond description. Families returned to the west coast for a depth of soil to bury their dead. The wrinkled coastline with endless tiny coves and a few small harbours gave access for fishing but new skills had to be learnt in a foreign environment. Overpopulation of the area contributed to unspeakable poverty and famine.

Curiously our visit coincided with a revival in the kelp industry. A new factory has been set up on Lewis and once again islanders are wading deep into the sea to harvest this bleak bounty which is now a fashionable item in health food shops and catalogues.

In the 1930s, as one measure to offset the effects of economic depression across the UK, a road linking the east coast settlements on Harris was constructed. It became the 'old golden road' because of its enormous cost. Snaking from bay to bay, it weaves the narrowest of tarmac threads between the shore and the tiny lochs with scarcely ten metres of flat or straight road in sequence. Whatever fascination the road might have for modern car drivers or cyclists today, the enterprise represented a vain attempt to retrieve a social disaster. Canadians now come to trace their displaced ancestors and the EU determines, with the HIDB, at last, to begin to repair the damage.

OVER THE SEA TO SKYE

Finally it was back to Tarbert – a good meal at a hostelry, settling into the motel box, a hard fought game of Scrabble, some reading and a few hours waiting for the alarm to go before our farewells to the isles.

The light and atmosphere often seem special on an early morning

The Shiant Isles seen in morning light from the ferry to Skye

sea journey. I found our exit from Tarbert mesmerising. The gradually diminishing view of the town, pinched between the mountains, and the rocky islands and headlands haphazardly strewn on all sides, held the eye. Soon however, the ghostly profile of Skye appeared ahead, with huge angular terraces and a steady scarf of cloud flying below the highest skyline. To the south we had last glimpses of the Uists in silhouette. Now the shafts of sunlight played behind the dark clouds onto the Shiant islands, like giant stepping stones. In no time we were skirting the shapely headlands of northern Skye and making an elegant spin on to the ferry terminal at Uig. In our enjoyment of the journey we had perhaps lost track of its significance; for all the modern, comfortable means of reaching these great islands to the west, they remain for us very distant and different.

Crossing Skye was the reminder we needed. The re-appearance of trees, even in small quantities, was a great relief to the eye but the volume of traffic and the challenge of towns were less welcome. On previous visits to Skye it has felt remote and, for all its exciting profiles, austere. After the Western Isles, Skye now seemed a relatively lush and manageable landscape. We contrasted the Golden Road with these expansive hill pastures and the comfortable settlements. The Hebrideans could justifiably apply the term 'southern softies' to everyone south of Uig, rather than Glasgow or Watford. Later, as we took a break at the familiar surroundings of Tebay Services on the M6, we looked again at the evocative photos of the hardships of past life in the Lake District. Normally these come across as severe images of back breaking toil in farming, mining, building, even climbing. Now, with the Hebrides, the blackhouses, the lazy beds, the isolation and the wild weather fresh in our minds, life in the sepia-toned photographs seemed a degree less stressful.

Visitors delight in the rugged, elemental beauty, endless peat, magnificent windswept beaches and the generous, engaging people of the outer isles. But we should not romanticise these wild lands. Life has always been ferociously tough out there, both physically and mentally, a constant battle with the elements and with so much unrewarding land. The ingenuity that the communities of pre-history developed to make life bearable is still recognisable in the dwellings and ways of life even in the mid 20th Century. Much now is changing, but the basic hard-fought equation between people and the barely controllable forces of nature is only slightly altered.

With every one of these journeys, I end with a determination to return, intrigued by a little learning. Some degree of their independent character is being eroded as the Hebrideans welcome more visitors on more air routes, bigger ferries – even now, despite protests, on Sundays – and more of the soulless, commercial trappings of mainland UK. Even the TESCO tide is arriving shortly. The islands are attracting small numbers of long-term incomers, people with skills and enterprise to add to the blend. Geography, thankfully, is protecting them from the second-home brigade. Tourism will generate more seasonal wealth and jobs but it is hard to believe that these proud folk will be content to become yet another cultural museum.

And should they trade their primeval landscape for those lucrative wind turbines? That Faustian deal is being debated as the months go by, but the councils in Lewis and the Highlands seem minded to proceed. In the larger context of climate change it will be a noble gesture. But it is truly crazy to sacrifice our ancient landscapes if we in cosy England do not simultaneously take radical measures to insulate our houses as well as Germans and Swedes do; and remember to switch off our PCs at night.

The islands at the edge of the sea are now, more prosaically, the islands at the edge of the European Community. Where will the balance of belonging settle? A unique environment is at risk; so too is the Hebridean community. It is the extraordinary people of the islands, as well as the elemental beauty, which makes the Hebrides so enticing.

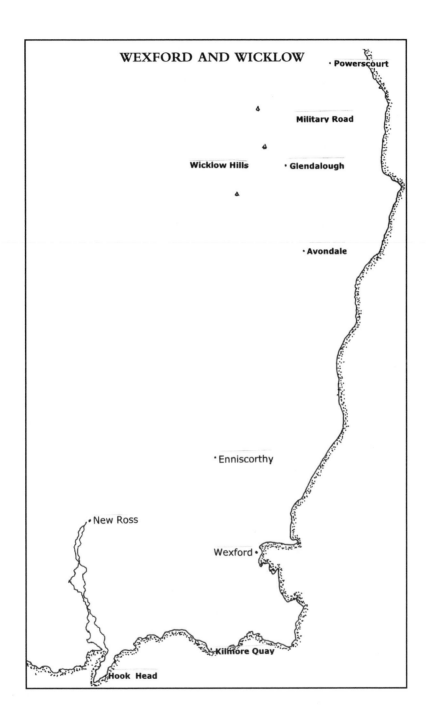

WEXFORD AND WICKLOW

· Powerscourt

Military Road

Wicklow Hills · Glendalough

· Avondale

· Enniscorthy

· New Ross

Wexford ·

Kilmore Quay

Hook Head

6.   IN AND AROUND THE PALE

AILEEN AND I enjoy travelling with a purpose. Even on the slowest of holidays, relaxing, reading, swimming, snorkelling, taking photographs, watching the world go by, we tend always to study the maps and ransack the guidebooks in order to explore. Some holidays are planned around specific interests – Cordoba, and the Cathars in Languedoc, for instance. We have also made research trips to prepare Aileen's visits with students, including Moscow and St Petersburg. History is inevitably part of such ventures but they are also about the connections of past and present, teasing out how communities are faring, making sense of landscapes, and, wherever possible, observing wildlife.

Ireland has become a magnet, endlessly intriguing and calling us back. Although we have no illusions that we will ever really understand the unfathomable tangle of the English in Ireland, the journey towards the light still seems worthwhile. There are few places on the planet where Brits can go as wholly innocent tourists; Ireland is certainly not one of them. Yet we seem to be welcomed more wholeheartedly here than almost anywhere else.

THE NEW IRISH QUESTION

This time we chose to explore Wexford and the Wicklow hills. Aileen has a deeper knowledge of Irish history than I but we both feel an affinity for the place and the people. We are still aware how inadequate our sense of history can be. The visual signals are everywhere; the landscapes tell their stories with unusual eloquence. The footprint of the English will never disappear. The long bitter struggle for Irish independence, with all its torments, and the famine, are writ large in every region and community. For the first seven hundred years

Ireland's dispute was largely with the English governing classes and the Crown. But in the democratic century the conflict became a dreadful battle of wills entangling communities everywhere.

George Bernard Shaw commented that the trouble with the English is that they never remember their history, while the trouble with the Irish is that they never forget it. So does the cheerful sweetness of the Irish people still conceal a deeper resentment? Is there a knowing self assurance that informs those smiles? New found prosperity, within the EU, has served to distance the bitter past. There must also be a sense of relief, maybe tinged with guilt, that the Republic has retreated from all ambition to embrace the north of the island. Perhaps that has left the Irish as confused as the English about the centuries of conflict. My sense is that a shield of pretence and forgetfulness has been spun so that people can enjoy their present good fortunes in harmony. This may not be an entirely noble approach but it is how pragmatic escape routes are found from many communal conflicts.

Our confusion was compounded at our first breakfast. We found ourselves sitting beneath the famous print of the leaders of the 1916 Easter Rising – all executed by the Brits –and looking at a memorial rifle on the wall opposite. Many cafes and pubs carry photographs of past heroes ready for military action. Such display is becoming more a token to the past than a potent political statement. But still a weighty reminder for we foreign visitors.

REBELLIOUS WEXFORD

At every turn in south east Ireland there are memorials to those who died in the 1798 rebellion against English rule in Ireland. In Wexford there is an imposing statue of the rebel leader. Other reminders mark the location of executions, sacrifices, and acts of heroism. Most of this commemoration took place in the late 19th Century as the wave of nationalist sentiment was growing across Ireland.

The 1798 rebellion drew its inspiration from the American and French Revolutions and from Britain's war with France. The 'United Irish' movement took shape in 1791, seeking independence for a democratic and republican Ireland through armed insurrection. 'United

Irishmen' emerged across the country, feeding on the plentiful grievances provided by Britain. They were the 'Irish with no property' and secured promises of support from the French. The explosion in 1798 occurred in 11 counties and lasted six months. Wexford's was by far the most daring and successful rebellion, led in part by priests and securing control of most key towns. In June 1798 Wexford declared itself an independent republic. On 21st June, however, a decisive and bloody defeat occurred at Vinegar Hill near Enniscorthy. Twenty thousand 'United Irishmen' were crushed by British forces, numbering up to forty thousand. Defeats followed in rapid succession elsewhere and the rebellion collapsed. Theobald Wolf Tone, their leader, was arrested in October, tried and sentenced to hang; he took his own life. The Brits then set about suppressing the remnants of the 'United Irishmen'.

Had other counties seized the opportunity as effectively as Wexford, the British might have been overwhelmed and unable to focus their response. Also significant was the failure of the French republicans to provide timely support. Twelve thousand Frenchmen sailed in December 1796, arriving in Bantry Bay, near Cork; but they were unable to land. When troops did arrive from France between August and October 1798 their numbers were insufficient to turn a cause that in reality had already been lost. The heroism of the Wexford Rebels and the Battle of Vinegar Hill became the stuff of legend, an enduring feature of the history taught in Catholic schools and treasured in the community.

ROOTS

Aileen was born and raised in the mining district of West Yorkshire. Her parents, like mine, ended their formal education at fourteen. Her mother was, in modern parlance, a carer for her parents from the age of about eight. She went into domestic service when she left school – not a happy experience –but became an accomplished cook. Given the chance she could have been a brilliant nursing sister. Her own family (and her parents) became the focus of her considerable energies and generous spirit. She wrote fluently, had an impressive range of interests and a quick wit.

Aileen's father was the youngest of eight from an impoverished family. As a boy he burst an eardrum playing with fireworks and was deemed unfit for military service. He worked as a bus driver and then a traffic clerk in the West Riding at a time when public transport was crucial to the war effort. This role gave him chance to study again through evening classes. Later he worked on safety and maintenance at the pithead of a local colliery. He read widely, possessed strong practical skills and could engage in intelligent conversation on almost any topic. He too was of generous spirit and had a quirky sense of humour. He was utterly devoted to his wife, sometimes to her exasperation.

It is hardly surprising that, given the talents of her parents, Aileen progressed brightly through her primary schooling. She struggled with 'number work' however and often found herself standing on her chair as penance for a poor test score. The problem was solved when she had to attend the health clinic on Friday mornings for sunray treatment. By walking slowly, she could avoid returning to school until the weekly maths test was over. She recalls just a couple of fearsome teachers and occasional resort to the slipper for boys. Her life chances were transformed by success in the eleven plus tests. Hardly anyone else on her council estate went to the grammar school, so it was socially isolating but offered the excitement of demanding learning – and the doubtful joys of hockey. Beyond this the idea of university was a huge leap into the unknown for families like ours. It was unheard of. Grants covered the direct costs but the loss of an extra wage coming into the household was a serious sacrifice.

When challenged about her enthusiasms, especially for the history of Ireland and for Russia, Aileen recalls that she grew up in a mining community which was deeply alienated from its English rulers. 'God bless the squire and his relations and keep us in our proper stations' was an old saying she remembered from her childhood. So her sympathies were instinctively with the struggles of those at the bottom of the heap who had been written out history.

She also invariably cites the influence of her grandfather. She spent most weekends at her grandparents' house, helping to look after the hens on her grandfather's allotment and sharing his delicious breakfasts of fried bread or bread and dripping. Her grandfather was a young miner in 1914. He volunteered to fight in the trenches and was gassed at Ypres. Though lucky to survive, he returned to the illusory promise of a land fit for heroes and to new battles with the coal owners over wage cuts during the depression. Somewhere along the line he became an admirer of the Bolshevik revolution and talked of the benefits of a 'workers' state' long after the shadow of Stalinism had destroyed the dream. He kept his views private but was convinced that we should not trust our governments or our 'social superiors' to tell the truth or to manage the world for us. Back in the mine, he suffered a heart seizure and never worked again. Aileen's grandmother also withdrew from the rigours of the world and the shame of 'public assistance', probably suffering from depression, leaving her little daughter to run the house. Nonetheless both grandparents lived well into their eighties, in a terraced house still lit by gas, with an outside privy, a coal fired cooking range. Aileen needed no museum visits to trace her roots.

Trawler's graveyard at Kilmore Quay. Nearly 20 vessels waiting to be broken up. Victims of the factory ships

THE SUNNIEST CORNER OF IRELAND

Arriving on the south coast we were, we thought, well beyond the Pale. After the Norman Conquest of England, Normans knights crossed over to Ireland and made Dublin their military base. England's interest in conquering Ireland ebbed and flowed through the following five centuries. The Pale represented the extent of English direct control, a partly fortified zone extending about thirty kilometres around Dublin. At its greatest the Pale stretched from Dundalk down to Waterford. Inside the Pale, Anglo-Norman landholders ensured loyalty to the Crown and to English values, looking out on a largely hostile Gaelic Ireland. So for a time the Pale carried a real political significance. In the 17th Century the phrase 'beyond the Pale' appeared, adding insult to Irish injury. Inside the Pale all was civilized; after that darkness. Such is the power of language and the language of power.

Kilmore Quay stands fair comparison with most seaside towns, including that air of unreality out of season. The small harbour looked impressively full, a marina surrounded by a host of fishing boats. The reality was sadder. Scarcely one of the fishing boats was seaworthy, most just rusting hulks waiting to be broken up. EU policies, responding to over-fishing by factory ships, have proved as disastrous for the small fleets here as in the UK. Wexford harbour looked more alive and prosperous but the smaller quays are rapidly being surrendered to the tide of marine tourism.

The landscape is not spectacular in this south east corner of Ireland but it does lay claim to being the sunniest and driest part of the country – not perhaps the most severe of contests. Defying a heavy sky we ventured out to the end of the Hook Peninsula and were rewarded with some frail sunshine. On an estuary, still shrouded in drizzle, a vast flock of snipe fed busily at low tide.

We were not wholly convinced by guidebook claims of the Hook Lighthouse to be the oldest working light in Europe. (To be fair, an imposing but ghastly mansion only three miles away from the Hook is promoted as the most haunted in all Ireland – so the style of tourist literature does invite some caution). The lighthouse really is a gem, however. It started life as a watchtower of the nearby Cistercian foundation, Dunbrody Abbey. Stone built in the 13th Century with lofty vaulted ceilings at each level and monks' cells in the walls it bears all the hallmarks of stylish medieval architecture. Austere as the location is, the house lately became the prince of Irish lights; modern keepers aspired to the space and relative luxury of the Hook, a telling tribute to its ancient creators.

We moved on to New Ross to visit the reconstruction of SS Dunbrody, moored on the banks of the river Barrow. The original ship, a three-masted barque, fifty four metres long, was built in Quebec by Thomas Oliver, an émigré from County Derry, in 1845. The construction was overseen by John Baldwin, who became the ship's first captain. In its early years it was a cargo vessel carrying loads of timber, cotton and guano.

Then for six years from 1845 between April and September it was pressed into service as a famine ship carrying impoverished emigrants to the New World. As the potato blight and the Great Famine took hold refugee numbers rose from one hundred and seventy six per voyage to an unthinkable three hundred and thirteen. Most of them were tenants from the Wicklow estate of Lord Fitzwilliam, a major landowner in England and Ireland. The same family, coincidentally, owned the mines in which Aileen's grandfather worked. The fare was the equivalent of about two months' normal earnings for tenant farmers and passengers were also expected to provide their own food for the journey. As the death toll from hunger and sickness rose, many landowners, faced with paying the mounting costs of famine relief, preferred to offer their tenants a one way passage across the Atlantic.

These were in some ways the most fortunate folk, who at least had some choices, however desperate, to make about their futures. There would be no new world for the vast numbers of sub tenants and landless labourers. The famine reached its most acute stage in 1847 when a gathering of forty ships queued to offload their tormented passengers into the overcrowded Canadian quarantine station at Grosse Ile, near Quebec (now an Irish heritage visitor centre). The records show the SS Dunbrody to have been humanely run by Captain Baldwin. Very few of its passengers died on the voyages under his command.

The ship remained in service until 1875 when it ran aground

SS Dunbrody by the quay in New Ross. A meticulous, full size
replica of the cargo vessel turned migrant ship
during the Great Famine 1846-51

off Labrador and broke up in heavy seas. No effort has been spared in the reconstruction, now open to visitors in New Ross. It stands as a worthy, dignified tribute to the shipbuilders, the sailors and the refugees. On shore in New Ross, close by the ship, is an excellent interpretation centre, offering access to documentation from the famine voyages. Many people who visit are North Americans researching their ancestry. It is difficult to balance out the sense of celebration at the admirable reconstruction with the sombre, terrible history it recalls. Smiles and tears come close together here.

BLIGHT ON THE LANDSCAPE

As we travelled we reflected once again on the terrible imprint of the famine and the exodus on the Irish landscape. The underlying reason for this is that, under British stewardship, Irish rural communities remained profoundly poor. The privations of famine, evictions and migration destroyed what little they possessed. Most 19th Century rural dwellings were of wood and turf. Many were razed to the ground by landlords' agents as tenants were evicted. By the end of the 19th Century this greenest of lands had used up most of its forests, largely for building and for fuel. England's countryside is full of cottages in vernacular styles, most now restored and coveted by the wealthy. In Ireland a thatched cottage became an unwelcome symbol of poverty.

Planning laws now allow anyone with an acre or so of land to construct a single dwelling. Land is not in short supply, except around Dublin. In most areas there is no dominant vernacular style of rural dwellings to give a template for new build. The result is a scattering of essentially similar, characterless, functional bungalows and houses across the countryside. We came across a book apparently by an architect offering for fifteen Euros 'All that is needed to build your own bungalow'. The contest for the worst new building has been joined by folk of more substantial means who have invested in high walls, porticoes, finials, baroque detached garages and hues of paint that can probably be seen from space. A dismal transformation.

**Traditional cottage in disrepair. Most dwellings were in turf and
wood, not stone as here. Thatch, associated with poverty
and famine, is still out of favour.**

THE WICKLOW HILLS

South from Dublin the eye is drawn to the Wicklow hills, a shapely,
green and gentle range rising to nearly a thousand metres. Settlers were
always attracted to the natural richness and diversity of the area. The
layers of history in the landscape are conspicuous. We visited a triangle
of wonderful sites, each contributing its own fragment to the Irish
story.

The first point of the triangle was Glendalough, 'the valley between
two lakes', where the atmospheric ruins of the monastery stand below
steep woodland and pastures. Founded in the 6th century, the monastery
was part of the flourishing culture which then distinguished Ireland from
its neighbours. The community somehow survived repeated Viking raids
only to suffer a devastating assault by English forces in 1398. Even then
it staggered on until the Dissolution of the 1530s, remaining a focus of
pilgrimage in honour of St Kevin. It has a distinctive beauty and is well
maintained, with an excellent interpretation centre. For all its vast acres,

though, Glendalough seems now in danger of submitting to a relentless tide of tourists. Choose a quiet time if you can.

The second location is a more subtle and less visited wonder – the Avondale Forest Park. The estate's Georgian house was the birthplace of Charles Stewart Parnell, a Protestant landlord who in the 1880s became the heroic champion of Irish Nationalism and 'the uncrowned king of Ireland'. Parnell campaigned for the reinstatement a separate parliament for Ireland and for radical land reform to protect the interests of Irish tenants. English absentee landlords took little interest in their estates, demanded unrealistic rents and ruthlessly evicted defaulters. Parnell encouraged tenants to take direct action against the worst offenders, including one Captain Boycott – a worthy addition to the dictionary. The British parliament thwarted Parnell's efforts. Then he fell victim to scandal when cited in a divorce case as the lover of society beauty, Kitty O'Shea.

Avondale House now contains a museum to Parnell. The Forest Park is the product of an 18th Century arboretum, planted in recognition of Ireland's need for more diverse and useful woodland. It has been managed since 1904 by the Irish Forestry Board, created to restore Ireland's woodlands. The desperate decades of famine and extreme poverty had led to the destruction (for fuel and building) of most of its forests. The sheer diversity and beauty of the Avondale's four hundred species of tree are incredible. The serenity of the park make it a gem of the highest quality.

At the third point of the triangle lies Powerscourt – a mansion which symbolises the domination of the Pale by the Anglo-Irish aristocracy. Built in the 1730s on the ruins of a Norman castle, its majestic estate spills across lush acres towards the strikingly beautiful Sugar Loaf mountain. The grand Palladian house had a chequered history, falling into serious disrepair in the middle of the last century and then being burnt out after a huge restoration programme in 1974. The ground floor has been impressively restored for a second time, otherwise little more than a façade remains. It is however the gardens, redesigned in the 1860s and regarded as the finest in Ireland, together with their compelling views towards the Sugar Loaf, that make Powerscourt so memorable. Like Glendalough it attracts a surfeit of visitors.

We then explored an even more dramatic imprint of the British

**Powerscourt House gardens looking to the Sugar Loaf Mountain.
English-style landscaping within the Pale where Anglo-Irish
wealth and power were most secure**

presence in the Wicklow landscape. Part of the response to the
rebellion of 1798 was to ensure that the hills would cease to be the
hideaway of Irish Nationalist rebels. In a tactic well known to the
Scots, the British authorities commissioned a high level military road
to control the access and vantage points of the hills. The circuit has
become a tourist attraction in itself. The sinister glamour of the road
in high summer's sunshine needs to be tempered with its exposure to
the worst of the elements for the rest of the year. Large barracks were
constructed at strategic points of the circuit and serious horticultural
experiments conducted to establish whether self sufficient settlements
could be created in the hills to secure them against the dissidents.
Characteristically, the British tactic was to populate the barracks with
recruits from the Irish countryside, a task made all too easy by the
prolonged agonies of rural Ireland in the 19th Century. What an awful
choice to face: sign up with the occupying forces or abandon your
homeland for the miserable lottery of the migrant ships.

The barracks now offer a more hopeful future. One is a Peace

Military Road built high around the Wicklow Hills by British after 1798 rising. Often wild and desolate even in summer

Centre to which groups from the North, the Republic and Britain come in search of reconciliation and an understanding of 'The Troubles'. Another is being restored as a high quality youth hostel, which will attract visitors from all over the world. Bring your sense of history to these hills. They tell some terrible stories.

MEETING THE RICH

Our final perspective on Ireland in this short stay arose from the generosity of a friend who had won a two day stay at a luxury country house in a charity fundraising event. His gift nonetheless triggered some uneasy feelings. This was not familiar territory for us. We tracked the place down with difficulty through one of those elaborate networks of rural lanes which are largely testimony to the public works of the famine years. Our modest vehicle at once felt an unaccustomed sensitivity amidst a competitive tyranny of Mercedes, BMWs and other seriously expensive cars. It could console itself with the company of the many delivery vehicles around the site. The hotel's own golf course

– impressively designed to competition standards – was wasted on me. In a blue bedroom the size of a tennis court, with a bathroom to match, our disbelief gave way to laughter. The bed was, inevitably, bigger than any I have ever slept in and was indescribably comfortable; so whatever else happened this was rest cure like no other.

The staff seemed as happy as any employees can be and were courteous without being unduly deferential; and this was not synthetic charm. They were mainly from the new nations in the EU, notably Poland, and really seemed to love the place and the chance to offer a high quality service. Too many of the guests, unfortunately, appeared to find the luxury and attention rather trying. Perhaps if you have too much money nothing is ever quite good enough. There may be truth in the old saying that wealth is no guarantee of good manners but we thought people would know how to try. So should I have been surprised to hear a grumpy gentleman being persuaded to take his hairy little dog out of the dining room at breakfast? Or to have to listen at length to a loud, inevitably trivial mobile phone call at another table? The food, like the service, was excellent without being over-elaborate or excessive. Had we stayed longer perhaps the place would have worked its magic.

SAD RETURNS

The journey back from Dun Laoghaire was memorable mostly for the wrong reasons. We reached the outskirts of Dublin early on Sunday evening with ages to spare and then faced a testing, tortuous, traffic light-ridden, lane-switching route which meant we arrived just in time for the giant shoe box ferry.

This time it was stacked full. Civilisation was in retreat. This was not about young people misbehaving. Nor, in truth, could it be characterised as relaxed enjoyment. Grown men were drunk even as we sailed. By the time we docked more adults appeared drunk than sober, most heading for their coaches out of Holyhead. The bus drivers must be masochists or paid Premiership wages to put up with this. Children, appeased with pizza, chips and chemical fizzy drinks until nearly midnight, were hurtling around like bats on a summer's night.

Parents seemed to have given up bothering. After a few delightful and intriguing days in beautiful Ireland we hid, depressed, watching an ugly world descend into darkness.

REFLECTIONS

Every part of Ireland bears some dominant, distinctive historical character and scars. In Cork it is the triumphant but tragic figure of Michael Collins who stalks the city and countryside. Elsewhere it is the famine and the exodus to America. In the south east it is the 1798 rebellion and its aftermath that loom large; alongside the emphatic imprint of the long Anglo-Irish ascendency. We understood a little more now, satisfied to have enjoyed a short exploration of this, the sunniest corner of Ireland.

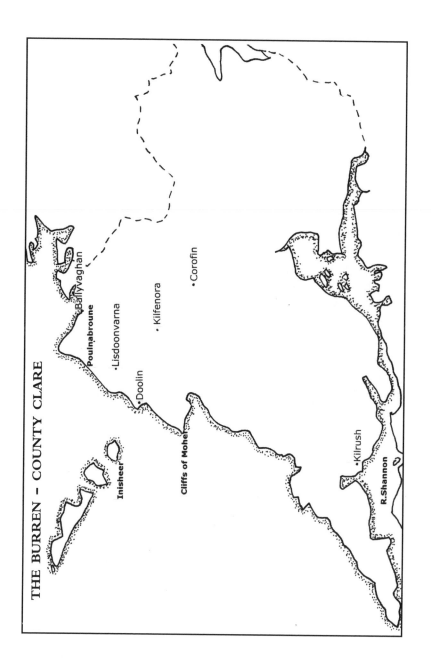

THE BURREN – COUNTY CLARE

Ballyvaghan
Poulnabroune
•Lisdoonvarna
Doolin
• Kilfenora
•Corofin
Cliffs of Moher
Inisheer
•Kilrush
R.Shannon

7.   COUNTY CLARE – THE BURREN

THE BURREN is a special place, austere on first acquaintance, but intriguing, and subtly beautiful. A lofty limestone plateau, covering three hundred and fifty square kilometres, meets the wild Atlantic to the west, Galway Bay to the north and green, gentle County Clare to the south. In spring the karst scenery takes on a multi-coloured hue as a riot of ferns and flowers, tenaciously rooted in the vertical cracks (grikes) in the limestone pavement, dances in the warm, long days. Mike and I chose the Burren for our venture, after many happy winter hours poring over guidebooks and maps. Its appeal lay in its distinctive visual and environmental qualities, in the layers of history in the landscape and the rugged offshore islands.

Mike is Irish but has spent most of his adult life in England, so this journey was a joint exploration by the exile and the foreigner into unknown territory and into our tangled national histories. We worked together over fifteen years and developed a strong intuitive trust which enabled us, in our different roles, to weather many tough situations. I always admired Mike's tenacious commitment to the well-being of children, even to the discomfort of schools or the local authority. This tenacity was borne of intellect as well as heart; Mike could hold his own in any argument, and persuade or conciliate his way through the most tangled of conflicts. We never made time for much social contact away from the demands of our professional relationship but our mutual values and views of the world left no doubt that we could conjure a lively and enjoyable week together in Mike's homeland. And so it was.

Our first stop after the unbelievably calm, early day, crossing from Holyhead was for tea and croissants in a sunny garden with Mike's sister, a wonderful welcome to Ireland. Mary's teenage children had, in early June, just started their three months' school holiday, so she was happily involved as mediator and taxi driver. Apparently the Irish Teachers' Unions defend this huge break ferociously and are very powerful. The parents' union, presumably, is not. Life in the Irish Sixth Form – a system more akin to the German Abitur – is competitive and pressured. Students are expected to spend nine hour days in school, with evening, weekend and holiday study as well. Conventional wisdom in the UK is that the learning of younger pupils can drift backwards over just a six week break but Ireland's standards are on a par with the rest of Europe. Enough of education, we decided.

FROM HERE TO CLARE

Plotting the best route from Dun Laoghaire to north Clare would challenge an accomplished orienteer. Although roads between towns are obvious enough, the longer journey does not readily emerge. New motorways and roads are being constructed across Ireland but our maps left us confused as to their state of progress. So we trundled for miles on a cratered single carriageway alongside a magnificent, but unfinished, motorway, populated only by JCBs. I took the bold decision, risking derision, to proceed broadly on a westerly compass bearing, using minor roads. Fortunately the minor roads were in good repair – and less crowded. We were seduced from our single-minded journeying by a small hand-painted sign offering 'Crafts, Paintings, Teas' which kept appearing at long intervals. So mile stacked upon mile; disconcertingly the signs reduced to just 'Crafts and Paintings' – not our immediate priority. Eventually, we arrived at the driest studio in the whole of western Ireland, a veritable mirage.

Our spirits rose when we reached the sea, with every sense alerted. Then came that first view of the Burren, brightly sunlit, shifting from grey to soft gold to white, and lapped by deep green trees and meadows. First impressions encouraged us more than the cautionary observations of the guide books.

Tourist accommodation in the area is plentiful but monochrome. We had settled on one of a hundred 'holiday villages' as our base. These are clusters of about a dozen new build, well equipped, white painted houses, grouped into a small cul-de-sac, and dropped into a lonely meadow at the edge of a village (or even the middle of nowhere). They meet the needs of visitors well enough but make for a rather sterile and detached environment. They are the product, apparently, of a Section 23 Planning provision, which allows easy permissions and tax exemptions for properties available to let for at least 10 years. So a tourist infrastructure is developing, albeit with a hint of apartheid about it.

We rounded the day off in Ballyvaghan. This is not a tourist enclave but an attractive community with a school, shops, its own people to chat with, a fine new tourist office, a farmers' market, and a garage. It even had an active anti-litter campaign to back up the new policy of a token charge for each plastic bag. In a busy hostelry we were cheerfully served by an Australian. Then we ambled onto the Cob to watch the sun set over a very low tide.

SHARED VIEW OF A TRAGEDY

In our conversations during the journey across Ireland, we started to explore our perspectives on the bitter, fateful trail of the English in Ireland. We somehow arrived at a shorthand phrase, to which we retreated several times each day: 'a mere eight hundred years of occupation and persecution'. Mike repeatedly suggested that I knew more about Ireland than he did, but this was far from true. We just had knowledge of a different character – mine from books, his from growing up in the culture – a valuable combination.

We both understood enough to realise how trapped each generation, Irish and English, became by its awful inheritance. The best opportunities to escape the endless tangle were thwarted by external events, especially the French Revolution and the First World War. Taking the long view however the inescapable reality is that the power to broker a settlement always rested with the British. When the Irish moved to regain some measure of freedom, Westminster governments invariably resorted to force to suppress the perceived threat.

For centuries an enduring caricature of the Irish – as indolent and unintelligent – remained common currency in the British press, politics, literature, and comedy. Even now it is defended as harmless fun. Too often it has been used as a rationale to justify neglect or repression.

The ghastly final chapter that convulsed Ulster for over thirty years in our own lifetimes cost thousands of lives. Endless efforts to find a viable escape route failed, such were the malevolent forces that had taken hold. The outcome is a messy compromise, borne of attrition and exhaustion, perhaps the only way out of eight centuries of disputed occupation. The inevitable solution – power sharing – had been repeatedly subverted. Now even the most obdurate warriors surrendered to the idea. Evidence of the recurrent tragedies of the peoples of Ireland struck us again, place by place and day by day as we explored County Clare.

MEETING THE BURREN

We spent our first day slowly traversing the Burren to give ourselves chance to develop a feel for the area. The character of the Burren is special in its geology, its botany and its history. The limestone plateau is estimated to be a thousand metres thick, probably bedded on granite. Over time erosion of the limestone by ice and water has created rhythmic fractures and shapes. Its innermost secrets remain hidden; very few of its cave systems are accessible.

Neolithic travellers found here a very different landscape and a warmer, kinder climate. It was forested, mainly with pine and yew, and had a fair depth of soil. Conditions were good, if not ideal, for settlement and the Burren became heavily populated, as the sixty stone-age burial cairns, many bronze-age tombs and over four hundred iron-age forts affirm. Over centuries the progressive exhaustion of the soils and the forests left the exposed limestone pavements of today. The Burren is remote from Ireland's urban settlements and is suited mainly to pasture, so much evidence of the ancient settlements has remained undisturbed. Many are inconspicuous and require an alert visual imagination to reconstruct and populate. It is, though, extraordinarily rich in pre-historic remains. The scientific analysis available to archeologists keeps improving. In due course we will learn more of these lost peoples.

We had read about the remarkable flora of the Burren but only as we walked over the limestone slabs did we really start to appreciate it.

This area constitutes one of Europe's richest botanical treasures. Seven hundred different species have been identified, including Arctic, Alpine and Mediterranean plants (I think we scored about twelve of these). Quite how this incredible combination of species took root and has survived is still little understood but an unusual pattern of agriculture has played its part in sustaining the environment.

The upper reaches of the Burren have traditionally been grazed in winter, mainly by cattle, which spend the rest of the year on the ample lower pastures – a reversal of normal patterns. Various explanations are offered for this. The Burren is mild and wet, with an average temperature range between winter and summer of only six to sixteen degrees. The limestone retains heat into the winter better than other upland areas. The calcium and mineral rich grassland pockets on the upper Burren are highly nutritious for cattle. However it came about, the winter regime ensures that the extraordinary flora of spring and summer are protected. In parts where the cattle do not graze indeterminate scrub overwhelms the smaller vegetation. This age old balance is delicate – and vulnerable to climate change. Tourism, for once, poses little threat. Most of the Burren is wild tumbling country, lacking prominent ridges and hilltops to attract walkers in droves. The honeypots that coaches and cars can reach with relative ease, are few and well managed.

POULNABROUNE

The iconic symbol of the Burren, on inn signs, pottery, books and tourist literature, is without doubt the portal tomb (or dolmen) at Poulnabroune, presciently translated as Pool of Sorrows. This site, off a narrow road with sturdy dry-stone walls, seems to be on everyone's itinerary and is pre-eminent among one hundred and fifty such tombs in Ireland. It is visually impressive, raised slightly above a rugged expanse of limestone pavement. Twenty years ago a major excavation revealed the bones of at least thirty three adults and children buried at the site. Radio-carbon dating puts their deaths between 4200 and 2900BC, – so of Neolithic origin – but the bones were not transferred to Poulnabroune until about 3000BC. The last identifiable burial was that of a baby in about 1600BC.

Poulnabroune Dolmen, iconic symbol of the Burren

In Orkney, the Outer Hebrides, here on the Burren, and through much of coastal Western Europe, similar expressions of ancestor worship pose endless intriguing questions. The best explanation so far is that the remains of ancestors were deposited together in a prominent position to oversee the well-being of the community and perhaps to ensure that the sun began to return from its winter journey. Belief in ancestors apparently yielded precedence to astronomy in the centuries around 3,200BC. Chieftains – probably the priests of the astronomical secrets – assumed greater power. Hence single (rather than collective) tombs were constructed for these 'royal' families. In time stone circles, aligned to solar and lunar events, were constructed everywhere. Many are tiny and difficult to find, others majestic and arresting.

We traced this revolution from ancestor worship to the royal priests of astronomy for ourselves. We left Poulnabroune to the crowds (a dozen at least) and made our way a short distance to a smaller, burial cairn – a family tomb. This was a kilometre along a direct, tiny path. Hardly anyone else comes this way; but we were crossing the great divide in Neolithic history.

There was still more to relish here. As we walked towards the cairn, the flora became richer and more impressive. The subtlest sweet scent arose from the crowded little gullies. We lingered to enjoy this beguiling place. We had started to discover the Burren.

CELTIC SUPREMACY

Just as we were beginning to understand a little of the historical landscape of the ancient Burren, we immediately came across another man-made feature of quite different significance. Caherconnell stone ring-fort is commendably protected, managed and interpreted by a local landowner for visitors. The site is one of many here, with likely origins as defensive iron age settlements. Caherconnell's visible structures date from the Celtic invasions around 500AD. The Celts moved through much of the western seaboard of Europe, but left a relatively light imprint on their landscapes.

The evidence at Caherconnell is unspectacular but convincing. It was essentially a small farming village, with an outer rampart of deep stone walls. They formed part of a loose, long term confederation of communities in the west which owed allegiance to the high kings of Ireland. They were also places of learning, craftsmanship and culture. The Celtic legal codes were taught here. Intriguingly the codes seem to echo some Hindu teachings, confirming Celtic origins from well beyond Europe. One fateful feature of the code was that land was subdivided as it passed from one generation to another. Major documents of Christianity were copied and translated, along with many other texts from ancient civilisations. This unremarkable rampart, like many others, protected a Celtic seat of learning for many centuries.

For such way of life to remain intact and thrive for a thousand years, is in itself remarkable. In the early centuries this flow of intellectual and creative enterprise contrasts dramatically with Britain's post-Roman 'Dark Ages'. It accounts for the missionary activity from

Ireland to Scotland and England. When King Oswald summoned missionaries from Ireland to Lindisfarne to convert Northumbria to Christianity in 635BC he was turning to the obvious beacon of learning and civilization.

KILFENORA

We turned to the Burren Visitor Centre in Kilfenora to check out our initial perceptions. Kilfenora was on its knees as a community a few decades ago when determined efforts began to turn it, improbably, into a cultural centre and a tourist attraction. Its distinctive historical claim is that the Pope himself is bishop hereabouts; a ruined 12th Century cathedral stands as proof. Now the village is renowned as a centre for traditional music.

Kilfenora plays a significant role in the Gaelic Athletic Association (GAA), founded in 1884 to promote Irish traditional sports and culture, in defiance of English dominance. The GAA retains a formidable influence on Ireland's national identity and integrity. Young people are expected to offer their first loyalty to the national games – and pay a penalty if they do not. Although Ireland is a force to be reckoned with in the international sports – rugby union, soccer, cricket and golf – Gaelic football and hurling are the regional and national obsessions. The GAA is still a massive symbolic presence in the identity of the new Ireland, as it was in the old. In 2007 the Rugby Union International against England at Croke Park, the high temple of the GAA, marked an almost unthinkable reconciliation, endorsed impeccably by the capacity crowd.

MATCH–MAKING

One happy effect of the Burren was to rob us of all sense of time. We trundled into Lisdoonvarna at 3.30pm ready for lunch. An obliging, if bemused, barman mustered a snack for us in the warm afternoon sunshine. Mike asked two passing local youths for a camera shop and discovered that they were two (East) Germans in western Ireland for work. Plenty of questions came to us as they disappeared into the town, but it does seem that Ireland, for so long an exporter of labour, has become a magnet for a young international workforce. Lisdoonvarna appears overburdened with hotels for a region in which tourism is still highly seasonal. Its peak time is the September 'Matchmaking' festival which attracts thousands for a prolonged party. This certainly beats the lonely-hearts columns of the UK press.

And then to Doolin, the famed hub of traditional music in County Clare. Unsurprisingly it was a fairly silent place at 5.30pm on a Friday. Accommodation has sprawled all over the nearby countryside to cater for visitors to the two hostelries renowned for their music and atmosphere. Our immediate target was the tiny harbour just below Doolin. Despite an offshore wind of gathering strength, a boat was heading south below the huge cliffs of Moher, the western edge of the Burren. The sea conditions were unusual and we had to contend with a heavy sea from the landward side until the cliffs provided shelter.

The trip was reminiscent of that to the Old Man of Hoy on Orkney, with an improbable sea stack stranded below the highest point of vertical cliffs. On the sandstone and shale ledges guillemots, razorbills and kittiwakes had booked into every imaginable nesting site. A few pillaging black-backed gulls were in evidence but at least the auks were spared the attentions of great skuas, the piratical birds so prevalent around Hoy.

We completed our initial circuit of the Burren via Black Head where the limestone pavements descend directly into Galway Bay. The harsh beauty of mountain and sea took us by surprise in mid evening sunshine. Later we were drawn down to Bishop's Quarter beach by the promise of a perfect sunset across the Bay. On the far horizon a few clouds gathered to thwart our expectations but it was time well spent.

BROTHER JOHN

Mike was the second of six in a Wexford family. All six have been in their different ways successful, four still living in Ireland. When Mike was fourteen his father died suddenly at work aged forty eight. The loss was so unexpected and abrupt that it still has an immediacy when

Mike talks of it; like an unfinished conversation. His mother's strength of character in bringing up the family, most of them through higher education, was of an unusual quality. She knew how to make each of them feel special but also how to uphold the key rules – 'No lies and no dangerous play'. She 'did a good silence'. I was moved to hear that as his mother neared eighty, Mike wrote to Mary Robinson, President of the Republic (and, incidentally, the best ever argument against the pomp and circumstance of monarchy) asking her to scribe a letter of recognition to his mother for her life's work as a feisty mother, worker, loyal Catholic, and unstinting supporter of de Valera. The resulting letter was duly read, a surprise to all, at her birthday party and framed for pride of place, alongside the photographs of Dev and the Pope.

Mike started school at three and a half. He used to go with his mother to take his older sister to school and one day decided that what was going on 'in there' sounded more interesting than being at home. So he slipped away from his mother into class and was allowed to stay, progressing early to every stage of education from then on.

The local secondary school for boys was run by the Christian Brothers, then a flourishing and respected order. The regime was routinely brutal, with heavy reliance on rote learning and the strap. If, for example, homework was to learn some Latin declensions, scripture or verse the test would be, boy by boy, to recite a portion in sequence. So did you try to play the system, calculating where your turn would come – and so concentrate on learning just one or two sections perfectly – or attempt the impossible of committing the whole piece to memory? Either way the risk was the strap, usually across the hand. Mike's recollection is that it was not unknown for some boys to be beaten twelve times in a day. Given the inevitability of punishment, it may seem surprising that anyone bothered to tackle the homework at all. The power of the teachers, especially the Brothers, was that they could invoke the threat of eternal damnation for the slightest misdemeanour.

Mike recalls the occasional conversation between his father and a teacher in the street, which would start with: 'Now is he behaving himself for you, Brother? Because if not we must knock some sense into him'. In a profoundly Catholic community, where education was valued as the route to a secure future as well as an instrument of control, the school's authority was sacrosanct.

Even within a culture of petty tyranny there were some teachers of integrity and accomplishment, with whom Mike became an enthusiastic student. At fourteen, prompted by senior staff, and persuaded of his own sense of vocation, he decided to join the Christian Brothers' Order. His mother was so proud for her son to become a monk. His father's response was more muted. Mike never knew what that signified. Three months later his father was dead.

Mike began his preparation as a monk and a teacher on the Wirral, then in Gloucestershire, as Brother John. Had he stayed in Dublin, he would have had to learn and teach predominantly in the Irish language. The road to a lifetime commitment to the Order was nine years long. Year one tested to the limit a recruit's sense of vocation and his capacity to fulfil the monastic vows. Mike then undertook A levels in a single year, including English literature. My impressions of that course suggest that parts of it could be quite disturbing for a late teenage, trainee monk. Mike assures me that the content was surgically edited to conform to the aspirations of the Christian Brothers. How sad.

As we talked I began to understand how Mike's sense of vocation enabled him to relinquish involvement in the key decisions about his life. He was nominated to study history at Cambridge, living within the closed Order. Despite his proven intellectual capacity, Mike was seized with alarms about the social demands of life at Cambridge. The boy from Wexford would be rubbing shoulders with the public school elite. An escape presented itself.

A Brother in Gibraltar was leaving his primary school post at short notice to take up a three year position in Rome. Would Mike replace him instead of going to Cambridge? So he was, after all, being given a career choice; and Gibraltar it was for three years. Then followed a posting to a Catholic preparatory school in southern England and the beginning of the end for Brother John. His sense of vocation was to work with the needy, the afflicted, the oppressed, for the well-being and advancement of ordinary young people. Yet here he was teaching the children of rich Catholics on their way, via public school, into the ruling caste of British society. He argued his case, which Mike can do very well, to be moved somewhere more fulfilling; but the breach became inevitable. Mike became a teacher in a comprehensive school, still driven by the same concerns as ever. He made his mark locally and then nationally as an advocate for positive management of pupils' behaviour. He has been married for thirty five years.

Later in the week I chanced upon a regional newspaper in a café. As I flicked through it, I came across a half page article– 'Christian Brothers relinquish school role to a Trust'. The Order has been so reduced in size by its dreadful series of abuse scandals and lack of recruits that its role as a provider of schools for the Irish state has been handed to an independent trust. A telling footnote.

ACROSS CLARE

We paused at the Ballyvaghan Farmers' market, which is small in scale but deservedly attracts a lot of custom from a wide area. The only fixed point in our day was a 2pm boat from Kilrush to meet up with the large, resident dolphin pod on the Shannon estuary. This lengthy drive would give us several options to explore County Clare beyond the Burren.

At the T-junction in Ballyvaghan stands a classic signpost bewilderingly festooned with a dozen pieces of directional advice and advertising. Today, however, an additional notice announced that the main route across the Burren was closed for racing car time trials on the Corkscrew Hill. Ignoring this first omen, we re-planned our route.

Our first target was the Clare Heritage Centre housed in a former church in Corofin, a small town in the middle of the county. It provides a genealogical service for those seeking their family roots. The centre has over half a million names on file and arranges, at a charge, searches, advice and guidance. Our interest was in the exhibition on the Great Famine of the 1840s which, by death or migration, stripped Clare of one third of its population in less than ten years. The exhibits bear eloquent testimony to a trauma from which Ireland, and especially its western counties, will never fully escape. As so often in a famine, the stories, the notices and the pictures tell of distress and despair more than of anger and blame. Over the next few days I started to gather a more connected impression of these dreadful events, the insidious web of causes and unspeakably devastating impact.

A moment of indecision in Ballvaghan

Somehow the call of the dolphins now seemed less important, which was just as well in a way. Around 1pm the Kilrush Dolphin Centre phoned to cancel the boat trip because the south easterly wind was increasing. Frankly we were not at this stage really convinced that conditions on the sheltered waters of the Shannon Estuary could be that severe. Later on we were to witness the wisdom of the cancellation.

Meantime in Kilrush, I inspected a memorial in the square which, from observation elsewhere, I suspected might be of interest. The architecture was, to the British eye, that of a war memorial. The inscription reads as follows:

Erected in 1903 by a committee of Kilrush Nationalists through public subscription from Irishmen the world over to the memory of the Manchester Martyrs Allen Larkin and O'Brien who were judicially murdered by a tyrannical government on Nov 23rd 1867 for their gallant rescue of Kelly and Deasy the Fenian chiefs from the prison van at Manchester.

God Save Ireland.

This was the first monument we had noticed in County Clare. The area seemed much less overtly politicised than Wexford, Wicklow, Cork and Kerry, where local participation in the nationalist struggle over two centuries is writ large. I do not imagine that the good people of Kilrush study their monuments any more closely than we in the UK would, but such events make up the backdrop of their lives.

Across the square is the town hall, adorned with an engraved slate, put up in 1966, in both languages, commemorating the heroism of the men and women in the 1916 Easter Rising. I sense that Kilrush, and the Republic as a whole, are confident enough in their identity and status now to wear their history – even its most bitter memories – with dignity; but the reminders are everywhere for those with eyes to see. To judge from the street names, the special gardens, and other locations Kilrush seems to have come to terms even with the Vaudeleu family, landlords of some notoriety in their lifetime.

We returned north along the coast road in deteriorating weather. The wild beaches, with their even wilder golf courses set against the dunes, did not encourage thoughts of a picnic and we eventually retreated to a Liscannor hotel for a drink. The south easterly wind was beating furiously across the small harbour and the wider estuary. Inside, on a large TV screen, England were reaching a merciful end to their colourless victory over Paraguay in the 2006 World Cup. Wherever this tournament intruded, we picked up a remarkably benign view towards England's cause – significantly less hostility than I have seen in Scotland. Mike was understandably more concerned with the outcome of Ireland's rugby test in New Zealand overnight. His enquiry to the barman and his manager was met with a blank stare and polite apologies. Both were Polish.

This journey presented our best landward opportunity to visit the Cliffs of Moher. A major reconstruction of visitor access to the cliffs was in progress, including an ugly excavation that will eventually give birth to a handsome interpretation centre. Sadly, safety requirements have determined that a huge swathe of concrete steps be built to allow the thousands of visitors to reach the cliffs in their high heels, flip flops and best bunny slippers. We were alarmed because at this stage the steps are but half finished and gave way to crumbling rutted footpaths along the cliffs. Hundreds were ignoring the warnings and inadequate barrier to totter ever closer to the eroded edges of the cliffs, buoyed up by the powerful winds. The obvious escape to safe ground, over a wall, was rendered uninviting by the presence of a huge menacing bull. So after a few photographs, we retreated, relieved that we had not been witness to any careless tragedies. (Some deaths had occurred earlier in the year).

We took pity on two damp hitchhikers heading for Lisdoonvarna. This personable couple, from Ohio, had embarked on a six month project working with organic smallholders. They had graduated in 2000 and were still searching for a foothold into their careers. We wished them well and hoped that Ireland would be their inspiration. It was satisfying now to return to the familiarity of the Burren, its mood shifting rapidly as the clouds chased across a confused sky. The coastal villages looked pleasingly secure, clad in protective woodland cloaks.

INISHEER, CRAGGY ISLAND

Sunday dawned brighter but still windy. Our plan was to cross from Doolin to Inisheer, the smallest and nearest of the Aran Islands. The

Irish wall designed to survive the worst of the Atlantic gales

tide was so low that we were loaded into an outboard dinghy from the harbour steps to a sturdy vessel rejoicing in the name 'Happy Hooker'. The American passengers pretended not to notice. (I subsequently discovered that a 'hooker' is a small traditional Irish boat). At last we felt we really were on the Atlantic. The HH pitched into deep troughs, and impressive waves collapsed into its sides. The rough journey took just half an hour. It was enough to push a few faces into green buckets. (Why do small boats always have green buckets – is it to match the faces or to sooth the eyes?)

I pointed out to Mike that rain started just as we set foot on Inisheer, affirming my reputation for inducing bad weather. Mike was reluctant to concede until the café owner commented that this was the first rain they had seen for several weeks. This short crossing is deceptive. The historical significance of the islands derives from their strategic position in Galway Bay, rather than their proximity to the coast of Clare. The reality is that the islands have always been difficult of access. These are Gaelic speaking, independent-minded communities with ancient roots and traditions.

Inisheer, a limestone cousin of the Burren, is dominated by a ruined fortress, and covered in an amazing warren of tiny fields defined by a million miles of drystone walls. To the east the bleak pavements stretch into the sea towards Inishmor. The scattered settlement comprises mainly modern, sturdy but unremarkable houses, with just a few traditional thatched, single storey dwellings in varying states of repair. A tiny 8th Century church occupies an enclosure just above the village, its dry stone walls and simple altar slab still largely intact. Ancient graves are just distinguishable as rectangles in the surrounding grass, giving the site an evocative atmosphere. The pub provided shelter and food, served by a cheerful young woman from faraway Limerick; more significantly it conjured up the unexpected miracle of sunshine.

THE GREAT FAMINE

We fought our way through the maze of fields up to O'Brien's Castle, a 15th Century defence set within an older ring fort. The castle owes its origins to the disputes between the O'Briens and the O'Flahertys as Galway's trade grew. It is a magnificent view point, from which the astonishing web of tiny stonewalled fields is even more conspicuous. In just one field, in the middle distance, was an evocative reminder of the past — a potato crop. The greatest tragedy in Ireland's history was precipitated by the frailty of that prince of vegetables.

Ireland's population grew from about four and a half million in 1800 to eight million by 1840, the vast majority of these working on the land. Dairying, pig-rearing and crops displaced sheep and cattle grazing, to meet trans-Atlantic demand. Potatoes were essential to break up the soil for the crops. The fastest growing worker groups were the landless labourers and smallholders with insecure tenancies. A huge class of subsistence farmers, often with little more than a sub-let single field, became dependent on the potato for their survival. It is estimated that 60% of the nation's diet in 1840 consisted of potatoes.

As subsistence crops go, the potato is one of the best in terms of nutrients, volume and ease of cultivation. When, in September 1845, the fungus *phytophthora* began to overtake the crop, a five year disaster and an enduring trauma gripped Ireland. (The blight also afflicted many other European countries on a severe but lesser scale of damage). Without the potato crop many families drifted towards malnutrition. They could not pay their rents without selling the essentials of life (such as chickens, pigs, and basic possessions) in a buyers' market and were driven into scavenging and fleeing their debts. High on the Burren there are deserted settlements where refugees died by the trackside. We were told of one property on the coast, where huge mounds of tiny seashells were recently discovered. Many Irish people have long avoided eating shell fish because it was regarded as 'famine food'.

Land agents, acting for absentee English landlords, moved progressively to enforce evictions, backed by the police and military. Landlords were taxed to fund poor relief for the displaced and starving tenants both in workhouses and on outdoor work projects. It made economic sense to reclaim the lands, assuming that the future lay, after all, in sheep rearing, not cultivation (just as in the Highland clearances). The 'Gregory' clause in the 1847 Poor Law (Ireland) Act stated that any family holding more than a quarter of an acre could not be given relief until they gave up their land. So the wretched dwellings – often whole villages – were laid waste to prevent the poor from returning.

Tiny fields created 1800–40 as landholdings were subdivided. Many families reduced to precarious subsistence farming in single fields as sub tenants, relying on potato crop

Many writers travelled to Ireland to witness the realities. The first hand descriptions of the Irish poor in the late 1840s remind me of those dreadful reports by Michael Buerk about the Ethiopian famine in the early 1980s, and many others since.

Many in Ireland who traded, ran shops, provided transport, owned enough land to carry on farming, or worked for government agencies, prospered amidst the horrors. Perhaps this happens in any major catastrophe. People cannot – perhaps dare not – show a willingness to help the sufferers for fear of being overwhelmed, so they look to their own interests.

Why did the British authorities not intervene effectively or wholeheartedly? There was no lack of first-hand information about the famine. Ireland had one hundred seats in the Westminster Parliament. Owners of Irish land sat in the Cabinet, the Lords and the Commons. There was even a fast in aid of victims of the Irish Famine on 24th March 1847, led by Queen Victoria. Writers travelled in droves to report on the tragedy.

Like governments of any era, they were muddled and kept assuming that events would turn in their favour, in particular that the potato blight would quickly work itself out. Free trade was the mantra of the day. Governments should not interfere with the natural (for many, God-given) flow of events. In previous centuries famine had been regarded as a natural phenomenon. Rev. Thomas Malthus, a leading English economist around 1800, had given intellectual respectability to the idea that famine was a necessary regulator to population growth.

More ugly prejudices also played a part. The common caricature of the Irish peasant as feckless, drunken and indolent was used to justify inaction. Why did they not sow new crops on their land rather than wait upon charity? (Possibly because they had no seed or stock and, as the evictions proceeded, no land either). Policies were shaped by such ethnic prejudice. More fervent Protestants viewed the blight as divine retribution on a priest-ridden, godforsaken country.

Many influential writers and politicians were convinced that Ireland could not prosper without radical land reform to stop the endless subdivision of farms and smallholdings. In other words, over-population had to be corrected and a new regime imposed on the countryside. Sir Charles Trevelyan, the senior civil servant responsible for the public works programme, wrote in 1848 that the famine was *'a direct stroke of an all-wise and all-merciful Providence'* ... it laid bare *'the deep and inveterate root of social evil'*. He declared it to be *'a sharp but effectual remedy'* which gave the next generation a great opportunity.

Even those who argued for sympathetic interventions were constrained by the prevailing belief that public moneys must never contribute to private wealth or relieve the landowners of their responsibilities. So public works could not improve privately owned land for instance by drainage or by planting much needed forests. Instead many useless roads were built by a helpless, malnourished labour force, who were paid too little to match the hugely inflated prices of available food. A growing impatience developed in England during the second year of the disaster – 'famine fatigue' – to which government yielded. There was resentment that the Irish showed no gratitude for the beneficence of government and charities. Added to which were the increasing costs of maintaining law and order.

Even the best intended interventions fell apart. Many landlords calculated that the costs and pointlessness of supporting poor relief were greater than that of buying passages on the migrant ships to America. Most of those who chose to flee were, however, the lease-holding tenants, not the hundreds of thousands of informal landholders and the truly landless. Of those one and a half million who emigrated, it is estimated that one-third died on the journey.

In March 1847 a huge campaign of soup kitchens was launched and is estimated to have fed three million souls by September. This was probably the most effective policy initiative of the whole famine; but it was intended only as an emergency response and was withdrawn in late 1847. The USA sent huge stocks of maize to Ireland; but its nutritional value was much lower than the potato. So it staved off hunger without restoring health. Maize could not readily be milled and was used mainly for gruel. Wheat was still exported from Ireland, although in much smaller quantities after 1845. Incredibly, oats, the easiest cereal to process and cook, were exported at double the volume of wheat.

The countless deaths that occurred in Ireland were the result of the infectious diseases associated with malnutrition – notably dysentery and typhus – as much as hunger itself. The 1851 Census records a national population of under six millions. The west of Ireland, the most impoverished region of Ireland before 1841, was worst affected, losing about one-third of its population. In County Clare the decline continued inexorably; the population in 1991 was ninety one thousand, less than one third of the 1841 figure. The Burren is sparsely populated now and much of the landscape looks untended.

Ireland's forests and woodlands were exhausted by 1850. The habitable housing stock was severely reduced; it is estimated that over three hundred thousand turf houses disappeared, through abandonment and destruction. The proportion of the population speaking Irish was halved by 1851. The economy, stricken by the demands of poor relief and the impoverishment of much of its population, was devastated.

Amartya Sen, the renowned Cambridge professor and Nobel prize winner, who was born in India in 1933 and witnessed the awful famine in his home country in 1943, made a lifelong study of the causes of famines, including those in India, Bangladesh, Ethiopia and sub-Saharan Africa. His analysis illuminates the great Irish disaster:

'Famines can occur even when the food supply is high but people cannot buy food because they don't have the money. There has never been a famine in a democratic country because leaders are spurred to action by politics and a free media. In non-democratic countries the rulers are unaffected by famine. There is no-one to hold them accountable even when millions die'.★

Blame for famines is invariably levelled more at its victims than at governments or those with wealth and influence. So it was in Ireland in the 19th Century; and so it is elsewhere in the 21st.

The British government could not alleviate the great Irish Famine because it was trapped in its own its ideology. Like most generations it had its dreadful blind spots. The 'laissez-faire' spirit of the time spelt disaster for Ireland. There could be no effective interventions to halt grain exports, to run soup kitchens for more than six months, to raise wages on poor relief to match food prices, (or to hold those prices down), to modify the astringent principles of the Poor Law, to restrain the evictions, or to withstand the 'Famine Fatigue' of 1847. All or any

---

★ From interview with Sen reported on Rediff.com Oct 15th 1998. His original work is Sen AK (1981) Poverty and Famines: pub. Oxford Clarendon Press. See also Sen AK (1999) Development as Freedom: pub Alfred Knopf (New York).

of those might have made a difference.

So the richest country in the world, of which Ireland was a constitutional part, presided over a monstrous domestic famine. It was not in gross numbers the largest famine of the time; between 1876 and 1879 in British India famine killed six to ten million; and another six to nineteen million between 1896 and 1902. Proportionately, however, the Irish famine was worse, with over twelve per cent of the population dying and a further twenty four per cent emigrating. And unlike the Indian disasters, it was heavily publicised.

The famine cast a very long shadow. More than any single factor, it generated a hatred of Britain that spawned and sustained the Irish nationalist movements from the 1850s onwards. The face of Ireland was changed forever. The Famine created the Irish Diaspora, committed for more than one hundred and fifty years to the nationalist cause and revenge against Britain. The flames were fanned by the failure to deliver Home Rule before 1914, the brutal defence of the Union in 1916, the atrocities meted out by the Black and Tans after 1918, and more. The Republic's neutrality in 1939 and refusal of its western harbours to British ships were telling acts of revenge. And then 'The Troubles' for thirty years – the final resort to an attritional war. Perhaps now, at last, the force of the furies has been spent.

BACK ON INISHEER

So there we were in O'Brien's Castle viewing the maze of tiny fields, which struck me so powerfully as a symbolic memorial of the Famine. We wove our way uncertainly on zigzag tracks towards the southern shore of the island. A cuckoo played its hide-and-seek games with us, perching and calling, then, just when we located it, swooping secretively away. Eventually, it condescendingly raised its profile to make it easier for us to spot. Then before us lay a large rusting shipwreck, apparently welded at thirty degrees into the limestone foreshore. This sad sight, a 1960s cargo vessel, has found fame in the opening credits of the TV sitcom 'Father Ted', featuring three wickedly caricatured priests, banished for various shortcomings to oversee the souls of Craggy Island.

Wreck made famous in the opening credits of Channel Four's 'Father Ted'

As we paused we were overtaken by four girls, aged about fourteen. In England, we would not have thought of attempting a conversation; at best a fleeting exchange of smiles, then quickly averted gazes. At worst they might fall into giggles, a huddle and a pretence at invisibility. The Irish quartet each turned towards us, said hello with broad smiles and opened a few pleasantries. Mike ventured: "So is this your island?" "No, no we're just staying here with families for three weeks while we go to the Gaelic Summer School." And so on for fully five minutes. The school covers Gaelic language and culture and the families speak Gaelic at home. This was a comfortable, open, cheerful, all-involved little exchange. How and where do these young people learn to feel good enough about themselves to initiate and sustain an informed conversation with two male strangers over forty years their senior? How do you grow such skilled behaviours and bottle them for export?

This posed a further thought. To risk a generalisation, the Irish smile a great deal, not in contrived manner but as a natural, communicative greeting that conveys how pleased they are to meet new people. To label this as the legendary 'charm of the Irish' is inadequate because that word is too closely associated with fame and glamour. Being greeted in a bar or shop or office in Ireland feels seriously different. There ought to be an international smiling index. The Irish would be at about 9.9. The Russians, who famously do not 'waste smiles' on people, would be at about 1.5. And the Brits?

HIGH TIDE IN DOOLIN

The sun shone relentlessly for the rest of our stay on Inisheer. We slowly crossed the long sandy beach in shallow waves and took up observation posts on the rocks below the tiny harbour watching inconsequential comings and goings. As the boat to Galway left the pier, the Happy Hooker appeared across the bay. The return journey was less turbulent than the outward one; until, that is, we closed on Doolin.

The tide was now at the flood and a powerful south-easterly wind was shovelling vast amounts of water through the three hundred metre channel between a small offshore islet and the mainland. As the Happy

The 'Happy Hooker' doing battle with a seriously high tide close to the craggy shoreline of Doolin

Hooker ploughed its way towards the jetty, it was suddenly at the mercy of a boiling white sea, with backwash from the shore adding to the main flow through the channel. After a rather drunken progress to the quay, the usual heavy ropes were cast to shore. The ring of old tyres and buoys around the HH felt inadequate as the tide lifted the boat hard and rhythmically against the stonework. We disembarked across a shifting gangplank. The tyres, time-served on the roads and now enjoying a quiet old age by the sea, groaned and screeched in protest. Maybe this is routine for the fine sailors of Doolin, but it seemed to us to be a bruised, unhappy Hooker that beat its way back to Inisheer for the night.

The angry seas had attracted a fair crowd onto the flat rocks below Doolin, watching huge fountains of spume and listening to the awesome suction of the sea reclaiming its wasted efforts. The contest between the huge energy of the sea and the implacably smooth limestone steps was mesmerising. Eventually we retreated 30 metres to the car, directly facing the shoreline. Simultaneously, but uncertainly, we spotted two black fins nonchalantly traversing our view, close to the shore. Dolphins were in town, following fish into shore on a high tide, scything swiftly through a sea that would have crushed any mere mortal. In seconds they re-appeared 50 metres to the left, then another fifty, pausing to indulge in some acrobatics, perhaps signalling, or cleansing, or, let's pretend, just having exuberant fun in a wonderful sea. We had experienced Ireland's Atlantic face for real.

BENEATH THE BURREN

Monday dawned wet and windy (still from the south-east). We had reserved a visit to the Aillwee cave for such a morning. The Burren has hundreds of caves, largely inaccessible even to the most adventurous explorers. Aillwee is the only cave open to the public. It is the highest profile tourist attraction in the area, which has a short visitor season; so commercially it is a challenge to manage. We were greeted at the entrance gates by the customary smiles and cheerful exchanges, then onward between limestone walls, overhung with dripping, verdant shrubs to the cave entrance at the edge of the tree-line below the Burren proper.

The architecture of the enterprise is imaginative and its educational credentials very good. But it has to be a tourist trap, adorned with tons of predictable bric-a-brac and kitsch souvenirs, alongside a coffee shop which adds steam to the ambient humidity of anoraks and umbrellas. Happily my specs de-misted for the superbly conducted tour of the caves, which had me stooping from six feet five inches down to four feet for much of the time. Bears hibernated in the caves up to one thousand years ago but there is, disappointingly, no evidence of pre-historic human use. Aillwee served to remind us that the Burren is, for all its solid, smoothed exterior, a honeycomb of lost rivers and caves that swallow with ease all that Ireland's laden skies can offer. This was just a glimpse of that indescribably dark nether world. It also reminded us that we are uneasy tourists, reluctant to follow the crowds.

SOLITARY SHORELINE

Expecting only mist and rain, we took ourselves that afternoon to Finavarra, a lonely headland by the northern shores of the Burren. It is marked to the west by an imposing Martello Tower, built as part of Britain's defences against the threat of a French invasion after 1800. We meandered along the easy path, seaward of a field wall, stopping frequently to listen and search for the secretive wildlife that owns such margins. By going so slowly we saw such a lot – butterflies, insects, rabbits, stonechats, wagtails, pipits, martins, terns, and other birds too quick for my eye to identify.

The rocky foreshore, gradually surrendering to a rising tide, was rich in rock pools and shells. Off shore a gaggle of cormorants clung determinedly to a long spit of rock against the tide. The sun's efforts to brighten the scene were at first feeble but eventually convincing. A flock of terns, resting on the water, became ever more agitated as the tide rose, swarming out to sea and over the fields, before returning to the shallows to dive and feed.

We turned our sights to a small hill just back from the sweep of the bay and devised our own route up the limestone, across a tangle of hawthorn and dwarf shrubs which clearly did not welcome visitors. Part way up, we came upon a level strip of meadow with quite deep soil and lush grass. Such pockets presumably help to make the Burren viable for cattle. It is hard to see how the delicate pickings of the limestone grikes, however nutritious, can fully serve the needs of livestock. The upper reaches of the little hill were seriously overgrown and although we were rewarded with a panorama of the Burren, we soon started to search for an easier route back. A handsome stone wall, running from the lane to the top, seemed worth trying, as we knew the gradients were manageable. We clambered and crawled our way alongside the wall, enjoying the challenge of the jungle, returning in good spirits to the car. This simplest of afternoons had been mightily satisfying.

The Burren had been good to us, its engaging landscapes vividly unveiling its past, and the gentle generosity of its people conveying optimism for its future. I shared an observation with Mike. As we journeyed, I had enjoyed hearing his easy interactions with his compatriots and, as the foreigner at the feast, had slipstreamed his conversations. The lilt, the flow and the joy of Irish conversations are very engaging. Trying to join in on the same wavelength is an unequal challenge. At times I almost wanted to play the journalist, pulling out my list of questions. I feel sure though that to appreciate and understand another people – Irish, Scots, Welsh – so closely bound up with the English, is to take plenty of time and visits, with eyes and ears open, mouth mainly shut. I will be better read and attuned when I go back to the Burren; it has much more to say.

MORE ECHOES

Our return journey involved another day's tacking across the middle of Ireland. We stopped at a bar in Athlone for coffee, listening in to TV coverage, and chat around the bar, about the death of Charles Haughey, the former Prime Minister, embroiled latterly in financial scandals.

We saw signposts for Athenry, which took Mike off on a little reverie. 'The Fields of Athenry', one of Ireland's most famed songs, originated as a street ballad in the 1880s (or even earlier), was re-written and recorded in 1979 by Paddy Reilly; since when over four hundred cover versions and over five million sales have followed. It is sung here in rugby stadiums, in Glasgow, across the Irish globe, and has even been adapted by Loyalists. It is the definitive ballad of the Famine. It tells how Lord Trevelyan bought in from America a supply of corn, in fact too hard to be milled. The locals thought it could save them from starvation and tried to loot it from the stores. They were arrested and deported to Australia. It is of course told as a story of lost love.

NEWGRANGE

We had resolved to take in one special location, quite separate from the Burren. This was Newgrange, near Drogheda in the Boyne Valley, a prehistoric site to match Maes Howe, Brogdar, Stonehenge, and Callanish. I had however under-rated what a visit to Newgrange might involve, and what the overall location signified. We approached across a tangle of lanes, came close to the site, visible on a hillside, and then were directed further away to a vast car park.

The impressive industry that is Newgrange has a purpose built command centre about one kilometre from the site itself. We were greeted with that unique Irish delight as if we were celebrated guests. Our coloured badges bore the time of our bus to the site. Fortunately, in view of our evening date with a Stena ferry, the delay was not excessive. Indeed it was insufficient. Apart from a civilised cafeteria, we found an exhibition of real quality, which somehow manages to tackle the questions raised by Newgrange in ways accessible both to children and professors of pre-history. This style of interpretation is intelligent and challenging, as at Skara Brae and Callanish.

A squadron of four buses left at the appointed time, each with its colour coded cohorts, to follow a variety of co-ordinated routes around the valley. We had time only for Newgrange but next time – everywhere I go produces a 'next time'- the place deserves a slow day. This is the Boyne Valley. It is sad that in the UK the Boyne is associated mainly with the battle of July 1690, so enthusiastically celebrated by Ulster Protestants each year as the occasion when William of Orange defeated James II, the Catholic challenger for the British crown. The battle site is only four kilometres from Newgrange but we had neither time nor appetite to go there.

The Boyne valley is one of the most spectacular Neolithic sites in Europe. It was chosen by settlers well over five thousand years ago as a fertile location with a broad river for water, for access and for fish. Across many centuries an extensive, sophisticated community of families have left their imprint on the landscape, most obviously in the great tomb chambers of Newgrange, Dowth and Knowth, but also in many, smaller, satellite cairns, passage graves, forts, enclosures and hut sites, all within a few square kilometres. Thirty seven identified sites lie in this small area.

Newgrange is a huge chamber, many times bigger than Maes Howe, surrounded by an incomplete stone circle almost the size of the

Newgrange: chamber entrance, roof-box and carved kerbstone

Ring of Brodgar on Orkney. The original chamber, from about 3,200BC, collapsed downhill over time and was restored in the 1970s using the reclaimed materials. At first sight the construction, with its white stone fronting, looks unlike any other pre-historic tomb but the restoration is authentic.

Around the tomb are massive, horizontal kerbstones, many carved with recurrent spiral themes. The interpretation of these stones remains fraught. Do they represent the closing down of the old year, and progress into a new one, or celestial images, or graphic representations of life in the valley? The association with the winter solstice is beyond dispute. Above the entrance into the chamber is a roof-box, an opening through which the sun (clouds permitting) shines directly at dawn on December 21st. Latterday mortals, in groups of a dozen or so, fold ourselves in half and creep along the nineteen metre passageway into the heart of the tomb, for a brief, but brilliant, explanation of its likely purposes. We emerged for a final look around at the valley before a prompt return by bus. A rock pipit, apparently

Rock Pipit entertaining visitors to Newgrange chamber

gripped by delusions of fame, perched close by on a standing stone for his public, goading us to take the perfect picture.

Newgrange receives one hundred and twenty five thousand visitors per year. The logistics are staggering, given that most people will go into the tomb in a group of twelve to fifteen for about eight minutes. No wonder the buses have to be on time. Yet this was not a rushed, processed tourist experience. It was relaxed, despite the military precision. I thought back to Aillwee, battling to attract enough visitors outside just two peak months. Newgrange, whose primary remit is to conserve, takes a full quota of people virtually every day of the year. It is amazing that the staff retain such enthusiasm and buoyant courtesy. It is also commendable that the entrance charges have not been driven upwards despite huge public interest. A magnificent experience, not to be missed.

Mike and I had left ourselves just enough time to meet the ferry. For the second time in a year, I found myself driving across every traffic lane that Dublin has to offer, repeatedly catching and then losing the signs for Dun Laoghaire port. I accept this as an Irish joke at the expense of the English visitor. Fair enough.

I learn progressively more about Ireland with every trip. Thanks to Mike's insights this visit offered more than any other. We wasted little time but somehow we never rushed; and for all the serious matters we pursued, there was a balance in the delights of discovery and of wildlife. A special week.

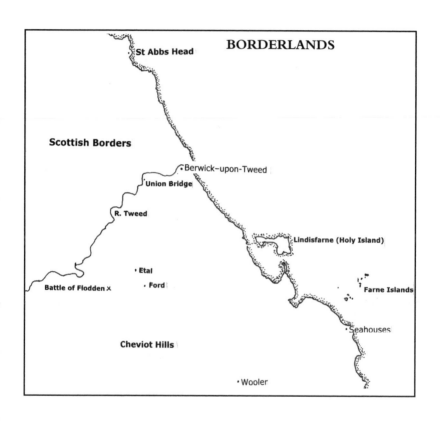

8.   BORDERLANDS

SEPTEMBER MAY NOT seem the best month to go to Northumberland and the Scottish east coast. The nesting birds have returned to sea, their natural element, and the seals are not quite ready to pup. But the enduring appeal of these borderlands – the beauty of the vast beachscapes, the wide open skies across to the Cheviots, and the dramatic histories – is sufficient in itself. By repute September is a kind month here, and so we found it.

The start of this venture was inauspicious. Shortly into my journey I abandoned John Humphries angrily interviewing himself on Radio 4 for the bizarre nonsense of Wogan. The traffic news broke any sense of well-being. A lorry crash had completely closed the M62. I stopped to warn Merton, in Leeds, that we might have a problem and to devise a fiendishly clever alternative route that few others would try. Of such are our dreams. Nearly five hours later I arrived in Leeds, safe but manic. Every vehicle in north west England must have turned out to enjoy the fun that day. An endless crocodile crawled over the Woodhead Pass, in both directions. Drivers exchanged good natured banter across the queues, shrugging and smiling wearily. Could we be forgiven a little schadenfreude that most of the breakdowns were those very BMWs that usually scare the wits out of other road users? BMWs are just not designed to move slowly.

From Leeds to Durham all went well and we relished an hour absorbing the solid beauty of the cathedral. Then on through a heavy sea fret to Berwick and a neat terraced house looking across the town to the imposing Stephenson railway viaduct. We shared the house with a few exceptionally large and vigilant spiders. These were knowing, inquisitive creatures which took up accusatory postures on ceilings, listening in to our conversations, watching our routines. We speculated whether they could they be trained for surveillance work or, failing that, could they pull shopping trolleys for older people?

Berwick has the feel of an important town, partly from its long, fraught history but also as the focus for a large rural hinterland. It has forever been the best ford or bridging point over the Tweed for armies and travellers along the north east of Britain. This location might have made it a prosperous port and city like Bristol, Glasgow, or Chester but it suffered the dire misfortune of being on the only natural border between the Scots and the English. So its singular fame is to have changed hands thirteen times in three hundred years in the Middle Ages. This extravagant tug of war was ended by the Tudor monarchs who encased the town in a magnificent rectangle of defensive walls, now restored and splendidly maintained, in effect as the town's parkland. Berwick now boasts four bridges – an early 17th Century fifteen arch stone construction (the last of five on the same site) low to the water, Robert Stephenson's handsome curving railway viaduct from 1850, an elegant 1920s road crossing into the town and the modern by-pass. Just for safety the town is now three miles from the Scottish border; but always keep an eye on the SNP manifesto.

Berwick-upon-Tweed: Stephenson's 1850 railway viaduct

So does Berwick regard itself as English or Scottish? Our host, a local history enthusiast, was slightly indignant at the question – undoubtedly English. For twenty four hours we tuned in to the local voices, unable at first to be sure to which side of the border they belonged. The best answer we could reach was that the accent is Northumbrian, the inflection Scottish, an appealing combination, and easy on the ear. By report, local youths claim they are neither Scots nor English – just 'Berwickers'. The pull of Newcastle seems greater than that of Edinburgh, however. (In early 2008 an opinion poll showed sixty per cent in favour of rejoining Scotland. Cynics suggest the appeal was more to do with free care for the elderly and the absence of tuition fees than an emotional shift of allegiance).

We noticed that the north end of the town has a prize collection of charity shops and more fish and chip shops than would seem logical or profitable. At the opposite end, in close proximity, all the Scottish and several English banks have laid claim to the most elegant town houses. Happily Berwick has not wholly fallen victim to the national contagion of identikit shopping streets. We tried to track down the common cappuccino. Our mistake. *'Would that be with aerosol cream, sir?'* A generational gap opened up. For Merton, *'aerosol'* conjures up his national service days when DDT was sprayed extravagantly over recruits to stop infestations. We declined the offer, stifling our reactions, accepting that we had been unduly conditioned by Starbucks and Costa.

MERTON'S STORY (1)

Merton and I have been friends since we worked together in Leeds in the 1970s. We walked the Pennines, Moors and Cumbria together in all weathers. Although we spent hundreds of hours in conversation, I had never fully pieced his life story together. As we talked now I realised I ought always to have been listening more carefully. His story, and that of his parents, could justify its own book.

He was born in 1933 to Jewish parents near Manchester. His mother, Sophie, hailed from Russian Lithuania, daughter of a boot maker, drafted into the Russo-Polish Army to produce footwear for officers. Faced with ghettoes and pogroms, they fled to Britain in 1905, settling in Manchester. His father, Henry, was from a long established family in London. Great grandfather, a vintner, had gambled away a fortune so the family re-established itself first as tobacconists in the East End, then running a hotel on the south coast.

In 1929 beautiful Sophie came to stay and fell in love with handsome Henry. But this was no fairy story. The cultural and class divide between the eastern Ashkenazi and western Sephardic families was profound. This quiet, religious girl had grown up in a traditional atmosphere, in a family labouring hard to survive their status as new migrants. Her husband, an engineer, socially well placed, enjoyed a more leisured life as a sporty outdoor enthusiast, especially as an angler. They would never have belonged to the same synagogue. The expectations of the two families pulled them in different directions and created tensions in the marriage that never disappeared.

Merton's early upbringing was seriously traditional and religious, overshadowed by anti-semitism. He remembers the arrival of many Jewish families from mainland Europe in the late 1930s. In 1938, as war

Merton

approached, his father's work took them to Leeds. In 1940, aged seven, Merton was evacuated with his sister to the home of a railway junction manager in Lincolnshire. The Stockdales, whose own son had been killed in a road accident, welcomed him warmly. The intensity and magic of the next two years had a major impact on Merton's future life.

The threat of a German invasion hung ominously over Britain in 1940. The Stockdales knew they would be at risk for sheltering Jewish children if the worst happened. Merton, aged seven, went to bed every night rehearsing the simple terror: *'If the Germans come shall I resist or surrender?'* He attended the village school and became a cub signalman. He learnt the ways of the countryside. At the weekend he went to church (with his mother's consent). He found the contrast with synagogue rituals, wrapped in incomprehensible Hebrew, inspiring. The lyrical hymns, the flowing liturgy with some of the finest phrases in the English language, and the previously unknown New Testament seized his imagination. The church gave voice, at that unique moment in the nation's history, to the fears and hopes of its people. The Stockdales had no thoughts of converting their young guest. Church was just part of village life. Little boys were expected to be bored by the services. Up to now Merton had been an outsider, a member of an enclosed minority, fearful for its survival and weary of persecution. Now he was included in a family and a community in the mainstream of English rural society. The experiences of family and village life, of school and church, and of railway and meadows were a rich mix. The emotional total of all this shaped his character and long term aspirations.

Merton's older sister, who had resentfully accepted the charge of looking after him, was mortified to see him so engaged in his new life and especially in church services. This rift would last for life. He returned to Leeds in 1942 to an all female household – his father was required to work away – mother, grandmother, aunts and sister, all programmed to wrap him once again in the Jewish traditions and community. Hebrew school five evenings a week and on Sundays completed the cultural saturation. A nine year old stood little chance of resisting but Merton had savoured a different way of experiencing life and the world, somehow more complete and liberating. A lifelong struggle had begun.

LINDISFARNE

By good fortune the run of the tides allowed us to spend our first morning in Berwick before the causeway to Holy Island opened just as a pale sun emerged. Known early on as Lindisfarne, the island was securely joined to the mainland (for eight hours out of every twelve) only in the 1960s. Even as the tide drops, much of the causeway seems scarcely above the surrounding water. The island itself rises improbably from the sea and surrounding flat land, such a contrast to the defiant ruggedness of Iona with whose history Lindisfarne is so closely linked. Undoubtedly the best way to enjoy either island is to stay overnight but we gave ourselves just a long slow afternoon. Holy Island seems able to absorb large numbers of people without feeling crowded, perhaps because its treasures are well scattered.

It has a significant place in British history. In 634AD Oswald, the Germanic King of Northumbria regained his lands from the Mercian invaders. He invited Irish missionaries, based on Iona, to set about converting his pagan peoples to Christianity. Ireland was the cultural beacon for the dark ages of post-Roman Britain. Aidan was given Lindisfarne as a base for the new monastic community. Cuthbert later became its inspiration, leading a successful local campaign of conversion and a wider missionary network.

A second revolution occurred simultaneously also with long term consequences. Cuthbert's conversion campaign was to Celtic Christianity, with its own version of worship and essential beliefs, and now at its most vigorous in its Irish heartland. In 664AD at Whitby, a gathering was held to reconcile the Roman and Celtic traditions. The Synod debates ended with a consolidating victory for Rome. Northumbria succumbed to the Roman rituals and lines of command, just as Cuthbert's Celtic campaign was reaching its conclusions. The Celtic church was now effectively confined to Scotland, no longer a force in Northumbria. Quite how ordinary Northumbrians, ploughing their fields and tending their livestock, adapted their beliefs and behaviours to this bewildering sequence can only be imagined. They were described as 'too stubborn to be converted' by the first wave of missionaries from Iona but Aidan and Cuthbert seem to have found them improbably biddable.

In honour of St Cuthbert, the Lindisfarne Gospel was

commissioned around 700AD, a fabulous masterpiece of early medieval art produced with extraordinary technologies and skills. The richly illuminated text is probably the work of just one man, Bishop Eadfrith, unlike most manuscripts which were crafted by teams of monks and nuns. The Gospel is held in a controlled environment at the British Library in London but an ingenious interactive facsimile is the centrepiece of a superbly designed exhibition at the Lindisfarne Heritage Centre. My doubts about the computerised substitute were quickly dispelled. It is a fascinating display that also demonstrates the techniques, the materials, and the conditions in which the Gospels were written and bound as a book.

Merton and I started to play with some unanswered questions. Just what was the central message of Cuthbert's Gospel that was apparently so compelling as to roll over, in a single generation, the peoples of Northumbria from their traditional religious beliefs to the new faith? Maybe it was the promise of salvation from hell and damnation in the afterlife. Or the appeal of the miracles attributed to Jesus and the saints. Or the concept of a benign god, rather than the controlling deities of paganism, always to be appeased. Or was it just deference to the will of their king and nobles? These early Northumbrians were tillers of the soil, shepherds and cattlemen, and fishermen, often at the mercies of the weather and the seas. If their old religious beliefs enabled them to make their peace with the elements and the seasons, they must have been reluctant to abandon them without guarantees. Whatever the truth, Cuthbert must have been, as described by Bede, a very persuasive and forceful character.

From 793AD onwards Lindisfarne was repeatedly raided by the Norsemen, who relied on a very different form of persuasion, and was eventually abandoned by the monks. The priory was re-founded in 1082 on a new site, itself ransacked in the 1530s by the English monarchy. The magnificently located castle, with its extensive defences, was duly built in 1549 and 'Holy Island' became an embattled stronghold during the border wars and later the Jacobite rebellions.

Lindisfarne has endured a vivid and complicated history. Its atmosphere reflects that. I found it less resonant of its religious origins than Iona. Modern Holy Island is unpretentious, just a large village of bungalows; sadly over half of these are now holiday homes. The island's

Lindisfarne: Henry VIII's fortress in background

stunning outlook compensates for its ordinariness. We set aside our ponderings on history and religion to contemplate the exquisite views across the sea to the Farnes and to Bamburgh, the seat of Anglo-Saxon secular power. What an astonishing place to have been a monk in the turbulent times of the inspirational Cuthbert.

BORDER WARS

Next day we turned our attention to the borderland conflicts, hoping for some convincing evidence in the landscape. It is hard to imagine the peaceful, empty, rolling pasturelands west of Berwick as a battlefield. Conflict is often borne of overcrowding. Surely in these vast acres there has always been enough land for everybody. Yet for almost four centuries neither English nor Scottish crowns could control these territories. In the vacuum, tribal gangs conducted terrorist conflicts of a ferocious character. They robbed, pillaged, kidnapped, raided, rustled, burnt, murdered, extorted, and fought with sword and lance. These were the infamous Border Reivers. Their visual legacy is ruined towers and forts, along with grimly familiar words such as 'blackmail' and 'bereaved' added to the language of Britain. The Robin Hood legend continues to romanticise the lawlessness of the Middle Ages. More brutal realities existed in the borderlands where common family names such as Armstrong, Kerr, Nixon, and Robson once struck fear across the communities. No King's Writ – Scottish or English – ran here until the later 16th Century.

Our searches started near the end of the story. The battle of Flodden Field in September 1513 is strikingly commemorated around two obscure hilltops a few miles west of Berwick. James IV's Scottish army of over twelve thousand men, operating in alliance with France, took up a prime position on Flodden Hill to face a four thousand strong English army coming in from the south. The English however stole across the Tweed in order to attack from the north, thus wrong-footing the Scots. The balance of advantage, reflecting the centuries old conflict, swung to and fro. Part way through, significant groups of Border Reivers, whose loyalties to the Scottish king were always suspect, abandoned the battle content with their bounty. English victory was eventually achieved by the longbow archers (incidentally the last great hurrah for the longbow). The slaughter of the Scots, including James IV and most of his nobles, was appalling; probably ten thousand lives were lost. On this occasion the cliché is justified: the river really did run red with blood.

The way was opened for Henry VIII, then Elizabeth I, to fortify Berwick beyond risk. The cost was vast, over one hundred and twenty thousand pounds, an unimaginable fortune, probably greater than the cost of defeating the Armada. Such was the importance of securing the northern boundary of Tudor England.

We were able to make more sense of Flodden when we moved on a couple of miles to Etal Castle, where a clever interpretative exhibition provides both context and detailed sequence of events. I had supposed the castles at Etal and Ford were primarily part of England's attempts to secure the border. The reality, however, is that they were the fortified farmsteads of the marauding border clans, which just occasionally served national purposes. We took time to wander by the fast flowing river, once more struggling to comprehend that this beautiful, open countryside had ever seen such dreadful and prolonged warfare.

LOCAL VOICES

To check out the picture we were building up about the borderlands we called on some friends nearby. It was a joy to see them again. Ruth is a border Scot, Ali an incomer from Alnwick, fifty kilometres to the south. They confirmed that, even five hundred years after Flodden, passions and confusion about national identity can still run high hereabouts. Some communities still ride the bounds of their medieval territories. Crossing the Tweed to work can still cause tremors for some locals. It suits many to claim to be English when north of the border and Scottish when to the south, if only to confuse inquisitive tourists. One litmus test is to tease out the rival attractions of Newcastle and Edinburgh – not difficult where black and white striped shirts are in evidence.

I plied Ruth and Ali's two sons, and their friend from 'across the bridge' with some boring questions about the history they learn in school. The results were unsurprising. At the Scottish primary school history is mainly about the Scots themselves, with some broader studies on the Victorians. They make a field trip to a battle site – Bannockburn near Stirling, an extraordinary Scottish victory in 1314 over an English army of forty thousand troops. The defeat at nearby Flodden, perhaps understandably, goes unnoticed. The tough histories of the highlands and islands seem to feature only as options. The English primary school, just a few miles away, appears to cover no Scottish history. The impact of what is taught may be limited but the messages behind what is included and excluded carry significance. I live near the Welsh Marches and I guess the same dislocation of history-telling occurs there as you cross the border.

Ali took on the management of a family farm last year and has had to push through some difficult changes in order to bring it on to an even keel. He is also, part-time, a non-conformist minister. So we abused his hospitality by asking how he would explain Cuthbert's capacity to convert the native peoples with such apparent ease. Ali is as much a teacher as a preacher; he works alongside people and celebrates their best rather than judging their worst. His instinct is that Cuthbert must have been a generous, supremely engaging character trying to apply the gospel to the everyday lives of farmers and fishermen – not an intimidating hell-fire demagogue. I do hope so.

MISTY BEACHES

After all this research our ageing brains were hurting. We repaired to the wild beaches south of Berwick. Sadly, the road into the dunes was bedecked with some abandoned mattresses, trolleys and other heavy duty goods. The beach itself was, however, impressive. Our hopes of sunshine were not fulfilled. The heavy sea fret, weighing down upon large pounding waves at low water created an unusual, theatrical atmosphere. It just lacked a few lightning strikes. The huge platform rocks of the Great Whin Sill, which cross northern England, emerge on these beaches. Diagonal grey pavements slice through sandy bays.

As so often, the beach initially seemed very quiet and empty, but as we stood still, scurrying seabirds started to emerge from the mists and soon we hardly knew which way to look. Oystercatcher, dunlin, gulls, cormorant and shag, a stately heron, and rooks, all subdued by the weather, took to their usual tasks. A solitary shag held fast to some slow rocks its wings spread wide to dry; not the brightest bird on the beach, it seemed unable to realise that spray from incoming waves was repeatedly soaking it. The heron, a grey silhouette against grey rocks and sky, kept a lordly watch over all the futile action, waiting disdainfully for the tide to bring the fish to him. We enjoyed inching our way across and down the beaches. Then the eerie peace was broken as families with happy dogs emerged through the fret. What a wonderful playground to have on your doorstep.

Shame about the mattresses.

ANCIENT ENIGMAS

On Sunday we set off for a boat to the Farne islands. The sky was bright, the wind moderate, and we were early enough to beat the crowds; but the tide was running against the breeze and the swell outside the harbour at Seahouses was far too fierce for boats to leave. The quaysides were swarming with human divers all kitted out in black wetsuits, like a parliament of crows, apprehensively watching the weather.

Our cunning alternative, worthy of Baldrick at his finest, took us to the hills near Wooler. Today would be a busy Sunday full of trippers – but not where we were going. The footprint of pre-history is not very substantial in Northumbria. However a late Neolithic enigma is scattered across the small hills east of the Cheviot, described imaginatively as Rock Art. Time for an expert eye, we decided.

We crossed a stile from the Golf Club lane onto a hillside near Doddington. Immediately we had to resort to the compass and some spectacles-off scrutiny of the (latest edition) OS map. Bracken and scrub had taken out most of the mapped tracks. The lack of fingerposts on the lane should have warned us. We assumed the Rocks with 'Art' had not moved and began a military style manoeuvre to track down the first suspect. A small cluster of large, flat boulders surrendered quite easily with two distinct, identical, horizontal carvings: a central thumb-sized cup, surrounded by three inscrutable rings. The location of the rocks was inconspicuous on the steeply angled hillside.

Our initial success engendered an irrational sense of optimism. The sun was out. Barely a kilometre to the second site, with a trig point as a pivot. We beat our way uphill on a hopelessly narrow track through the bracken. An early triumph took us to a stile over a spiteful barbed wire fence – but into ever deepening bracken. I had the advantage of a line of sight to the brow of the hill. Merton, several inches shorter, trustingly followed in the dark trough I was ploughing slowly through the high vegetation. *'Curse this damned jungle, Carruthers'* he muttered. A path of sorts met us as we reached the top. The shallow ramparts of an iron-age settlement could just be traced in the bracken. Then came our reward – the trig point. Now it would be easy. We only had to find the wide track marked unmistakably on the OS map. If only.

The lie of the land was unhelpfully steep. The path had disappeared beneath heather and bilberries. The golf course had expanded into the hillside, planting cantilever tees into the slope. At times we skulked along the edge of the greens scrutinising various rocks above us. None revealed any carvings, even to the most gullible imagination. My shins were numb with dragging against the bracken. After several vain attempts we retreated.

On another lane, and another hillside (Weetwood) our fortunes changed. First, a signpost to offer hope of a path. Then some scythed clearances in the bracken, and tiny cairns marking about eight sets of carvings within a thirty metre radius. These were all horizontal, some to the same pattern as Doddington, others just a larger cup joined to a smaller one by a short channel. Erosion had taken more of a toll here. Again the location was enigmatic. The rocks were part way up an indeterminate slope, hardly an obvious territory marker or tribal signature.

Nearby, in Fowberry, we found a further cluster of carvings, even closer together. As at Weetwood there was some variation in design but the essential cup, with outer rings or an adjacent smaller hollow, remained decipherable. Here also were some small vertical rock faces – but uncarved. If the purpose was 'Art' would not someone have used these faces for display?

Our sample of these carvings was tiny in relation to the hundreds in Northumberland. Durham, Yorkshire (Ilkley Moor), Scotland and Ireland also carry similar decoration from ancient peoples; but hardly any occur in the south. For what it is worth we argued out our conclusions. The carvings we saw were all more or less horizontal, which suggests they might have been meant to hold liquid. The locations tell of secrecy rather than signalling. We could not see much connection between the different sites. There is no consistent pattern of compass alignment. They stand at between one hundred and one hundred and seventy metres. The clustering of carvings does not fit well with ideas of sacrificial or sacred sites. If this is art, why is it so repetitive and what aspect of Neolithic life does it represent? The absence (of evidence) of settlements contemporary with the carvings is hard to explain. More likely these carvings were by or for travellers on now untraceable routeways.

Our best effort to explain these markings? Could they have been used for the mixing of medicines, hallucinatory potions such as fungi and herbs or sedatives for spear tips when preparing to hunt? If the area really did have so few settlements, then were these sites for the mysterious benefit of hunting parties, traders or others travellers? Apologies to anyone hoping for some cosmic explanations; but everyone is free to invent their own. A research project run jointly by the county council and English Heritage is now in train. We will cheerfully concede to its outcomes.

OTTER SPOTTING (1)

Towards dusk we took up a lookout position below the Union Bridge high above the Tweed. This is an elegant suspension bridge, built in 1820 to join England and Scotland in meadowland a few miles west of Berwick. It now carries one car at a time and bounces rhythmically with each crossing. We had been told that this was a likely place to see otters at dawn or dusk. It was a magical hour. The broad, powerful flow of the river creates an atmosphere of its own. Large numbers of birds came to the woodland to roost, their noise gradually dropping, then building again and finally dying away. Rather like excited children in a dormitory on a school trip, the last word is never reached. Some pigeon, rook, starling or duck topples from its bunk and they all start shouting again. Six swans drifted effortlessly downstream in the near dark. The heron, having superintended the messy end to another day retreated to its roost for the night. If the otters ever came, we missed them.

MERTON'S STORY (2)

In 1944 Merton started secondary school at Roundhay, on the same day as the young Alan Bennett was making his way to nearby Lawnswood. Roundhay had a strong Jewish cohort whose identity was affirmed in their own daily assembly led not by staff or a rabbi but by sixth form boys. Merton was ill at ease in these gatherings, which were used to promote Zionism, and to browbeat pupils into raising money for groups who were buying land from Palestinians and guns to fight for emergent Israel. He shared the dream of a safe haven for Jews but with international, not sectarian, credentials. Was the end of this dreadful war merely to presage the start of another? He attributes his sense of alienation, of a different vision, to his years in Lincolnshire. I read it as part of his essential gentleness of spirit.

A Jewish school within a school was reinforced by attendance at Synagogue, by the Jewish scout group (both leaders waiting to migrate to Israel), by exclusion from school teams on Saturday mornings, by the ordeal of Bar Mitzvah, and a tightly controlled social circle. Escape routes did not really exist, especially at a time when deference and conformity were taken for granted.

National Service did not of itself offer liberation. The religion of recruits was identified on their neck tags and assumed unreasonable importance. Merton recognises in retrospect the moment of his demob in 1954 as a turning point. Or rather a returning point. He went back instinctively – if reluctantly – to the family web in Leeds. He was being primed to manage his uncle's manufacturing business. He may have lacked intuitive financial and business acumen; but his essential flaw was that he did not think or behave like an industrial boss, finding his natural friends among craftsmen whose skills he admired. The extended family offered an alternative, more promising, line of employment in London.

Then followed the greatest crime a Jewish son could commit. He fell in love with an Australian girl who was not Jewish. His mother's family pride would not be brooked. She let it be known that if he married out they would conduct his funeral service and cut him off totally from the family. He found out much later that the family secretly paid his girlfriend extravagantly to leave for America. Merton still feels deeply the hurt and humiliation of those few months. I shared his anger at this ghastly manipulation at the hands of his family. We reminded ourselves that this was 1958 when the power of parents, Jewish, Christian or agnostic, was still formidable. At least Merton now took control of his career and by stealth switched his allegiance to the Anglicanism of his brief childhood. Nonetheless he was duly steered into a predictably difficult Jewish marriage, which lasted 15 years. We ruefully wondered whether Woody Allen was searching for a new script.

Merton then had the good fortune, quite by chance, to meet Gill, another Australian, also in recovery from a broken marriage. Whatever went before, and whatever hurt remains, they seem to be well suited, very caring and contented. I was around in some of Merton's darkest days and it always pleases me to see them together. For the last several years they have taken long summer holidays in a remote, simple gite in deepest rural France. Merton always contrives to send a post card of such obscurity (for example sheep in field, stone wall, tree in mist) as to give no clue about their location. Is he worried I might just drop in?

The really happy ending to all this is that this next Jewish generation – Merton's children and many others like them – are making their own decisions about their life partners and their careers. Young people in the Asian communities are going through similar agonies now. Such liberation takes time and determination.

(This story and our reflections can be verified by the ever attentive pair of spiders, listening in from their ceiling encampment.)

THE FARNE ISLANDS

At the second attempt we embarked on a tour of the Farne Islands. We took some juvenile pleasure at claiming a position standing at the deep prow of the boat which gave us excellent views. Initially the sea was benign, later more turbulent; but there was little hint of the wildness that helped shape these little islands. As expected most of the nesting birds had retreated to their natural environment in open water. The seals however were gathered in large numbers, ready to give birth in October, insatiably curious and playful.

Over the centuries the Farnes attracted many hermits, notably St Cuthbert himself. A monastic settlement was established in the 9th Century, part of whose role was to light beacons to warn off passing vessels. The coast is notorious for its sea frets and fogs, so inevitably the Farnes have been a graveyard for ships. A series of Lights were built from 1673 onwards but it proved difficult to find the best locations amidst such a scattering of tiny islands. In 1826 the famed Longstone Light was constructed on the outermost island with stone quarried in Yorkshire. William Darling was paid seventy pounds a year to keep the

Shag drying, preening, sharing news near Farnes

Light. He also benefited from shooting and fishing rights and, more lucratively, from the salvaging of wrecks.

On September 5th 1838 The Forfarshire, a steamer rigged for sail, left Hull for Dundee with a cargo of cloth and hardware, a crew of twenty four with thirty nine passengers. The boilers failed off St Abbs' Head and the vessel made sail south to seek shelter by Inner Farne. In the early hours of 7th September, against huge seas and gale force winds, the captain confused the two Lights on the Farnes and drove his vessel onto rocks south of the Longstone. William Darling and his daughter Grace twice rowed to the wreck, rescuing nine survivors. The North Sunderland lifeboat arrived shortly after and a dispute ensued with William, presumably over salvage rights. Press reports greatly exaggerated Grace Darling's deeds; but she deservedly became a national hero and received seven hundred pounds (including fifty from the Queen) from the public, along with gifts and proposals of marriage. Sadly she died of TB in 1842, aged just twenty six.

The sea was wilder on the way back but hardly enough to conjure any idea of what Grace Darling faced in September one hundred and seventy years earlier. We stumbled windswept along the quay. The weather was promising enough to draw us into a journey north to St Abb's Head, a magnificent promontory and yet another protected by the National Trust. A glorious switchback path leads to yet another lighthouse. We perched ourselves on a small grassy headland, watching a small boat checking lobster pots, while gannets dived high and deep and terns dipped with style. I have no idea why some gannets stay behind when most take to the open sea, but I was delighted at the entertainment they offered us. This was perhaps a strange backdrop for us to reflect on my theme of 'the most favoured generation' but the conversation, once lit, was unstoppable.

MERTON'S PERSPECTIVE

As I started to rehearse this recurrent theme of the uniquely fortunate post-war generation, I realised that Merton really did not belong to it. As

St Abb's Head: Lobster boat checking pots

he gently pointed out, to be born in the great depression, as the Nazis took power in Germany and to be evacuated aged seven under threat of invasion and persecution for being Jewish, was hardly the most fortunate early childhood. 1945 had a different significance for him. The allied victory promised so much, even against the emerging horrors of the holocaust and Stalin's atrocities. This was a triumph of humanity over racist oppression, of democracy over tyranny. Surely the world would now be determined to resist any such threats to the lives of ordinary people? Merton as a teenager despaired to see such hopes fall apart so quickly.

The international community failed to find a powerful voice as the muscle-bound military alliances and self-serving national governments held sway. Merton still feels impassioned about the endless failures effectively to confront genocides and racist tyranny. It will be forever to our shame that so many governments, even into the 1980s, gave succour to the apartheid regime. Worst of all for Merton is to witness Israel's progressive militarism and oppression of the Palestinians. The dreams and hopes of 1945 turned into many a nightmare. The sense of terror in his early years gives his perspective a moving intensity. We who were born after the war are innocents by comparison.

Perhaps it was as well that we ventured along these troubled avenues while sitting in such an idyllic spot overlooking a wild sea. The repeated distractions of the diving, twisting gannets, scoring full marks at the Olympics every time, helped us to relish our sombre reflections. I felt I had at last heard Merton's story and appreciated, for all his generous interest in others and his quiet intellect and wit, that he has carried more burdens than anyone guessed.

OTTER SPOTTING (2)

The day, and our journey, ended with a return to the Union Bridge as dusk approached, this time cowering on the parapet itself against a cold wind. The river scene is enticing enough as day ends, so we were prepared to wait for a while before retreating. I had just (rather belatedly) warned Merton that my record as the world's least successful otter spotter has been hard earned. Then he waved me across pointing downstream to some strange movement in the water one hundred and fifty metres away. The binoculars confirmed that two otters were swirling through the dusk towards us close to the river bank. They were approaching a large patch of lily pads before we realised that one of the otters had become two – young ones swimming so closely around each other that they could hardly be distinguished.

The mother struck with great speed and surprise, seizing a duck from beneath the lily pads. The tormented squealing lasted perhaps for a minute, piercing the silence. Most of the young ducks gathered into a tight scrum on the lily pads around their mother. Others, as happens in duck society, were excluded from this secure corral and were left scurrying for safety whenever one of the otters re-emerged. Even the statuesque heron deigned to move onto the bank away from the threat. An episode raw in tooth and claw.

I discovered afterwards that river otters generally swim with the stream each morning and upstream at dusk. The young are born usually in April and are weaned by four months. So these two were probably still in training – playing while the parent provided supper. They disappeared from view as the light finally faded, probably into their lair beneath the thick undergrowth on the bank.

A memorable end to the journey.

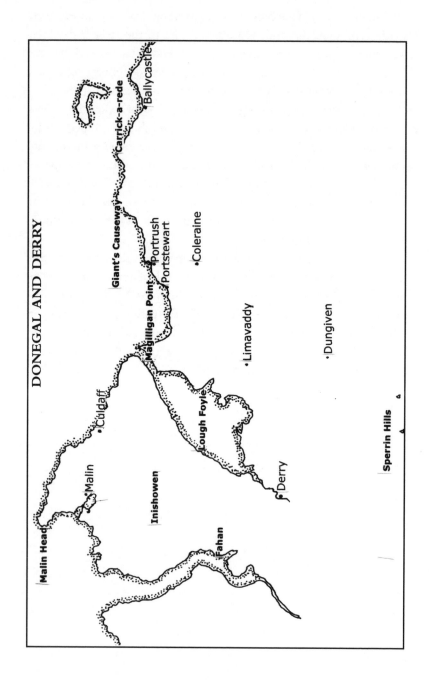

DONEGAL AND DERRY

9.   IRELAND ACROSS THE DIVIDE

LATE APRIL 2007 was a wonderful time to venture into the north of Ireland, with the sectarian arch-enemies just hours away from joining forces in a power sharing executive. Never say 'never, never, never'. We found people ready to discard their hard-earned cynicism and seized with a relaxed optimism. Almost as remarkable, not a drop of rain fell in our six day visit; the sun shone in mostly cloudless skies. As if that was not enough, on our fourth day smoking in public places was banned.

Helmut and I met at Atlantic College four decades ago. Our long friendship has relied unduly on his exceptional command of English, as against my barely adequate German. He taught English inspirationally in a Gymnasium for over thirty years and loves much about Britain. With sixth-form students he has, year on year, tackled "The Irish Question". So we both came to this part of Ireland with sufficient understanding to ask some of the right questions and a readiness to learn.

We also chose this destination for the famed beauty of the Antrim and Donegal coasts. I had to remind myself how easy it is for us in Britain to take seascapes for granted and how compelling these coasts are for so many in landlocked continental Europe. Helmut delights in the excitement of coastal scenery, the freshness of the air and the visual surprises. This region is also unusual because tourism has endured such a prolonged and troubled infancy. Even now we came across few English visitors. The infrastructure is growing slowly. The trickle will become a flood soon enough. Go now, while it is quiet.

DUNGIVEN

Our hosts were dairy farmers near Dungiven who have, with EU grants, converted their fold-yard buildings to very high standard accommodation at reasonable rents – a model for others to follow. The family traces its roots here to the 17th Century plantations, whereby the English Crown distributed Catholic land to loyal Protestant families from the mainland. Dungiven, a bustling, unpretentious settlement of barely three thousand, remains almost entirely Catholic and was a Republican stronghold throughout the 'Troubles'. Sinn Fein has an office amidst the run of small shops along the town street. Three soldiers were blown up here by an IRA landmine in 1972 and a monument commemorates Kevin Lynch who died as a hunger striker in 1981. Daily life was routinely disrupted by the menace of minor incidents. Such days are gone, but not, in this generation, forgotten.

THE ANTRIM COAST

Our first day dawned with brilliant sun so we agreed to treat ourselves to the tourist route along the Antrim coast. This was the first real test for Helmut the Navigator. He succumbed to a surfeit of Ballys – Ballymoney, Ballycastle, Ballybogy, Ballyrashane, Ballylintagh and Ballyeverywhere – which took us slightly astray. I also distracted him by remembering that, sixteen hours into our venture, I had still not asked him for the latest news about Knut, The People's Polar Bear Cub in Berlin Zoo. His response was reassuring. Attention had in fact turned to the excessive antics of the overseas media rather than the cub himself.

This is rich farmland, with large meadows bordered by hedges and with endless tracts of gorse in full bloom. It might, at a casual viewing, be rural southern England, but we observed that there are very few village communities – houses, pub, church, school; rather a scattering of mainly modern farms and dwellings. A few handsome older houses remain and an occasional stone cottage of humbler origin, often semi-derelict. The mainland fashion for restoration of these has still not taken hold here.

After our slightly meandering route to the coast we found the seafront at Ballycastle to be a surprising delight, especially remembering that the town grew as an industrial centre, not a resort.

We were lured, like good tourists, to the Carrick-a-Rede rope bridge, star turn of the 'Come to Northern Ireland' advertisements. Visually it is every bit as arresting as we had hoped and the location is stunning. However the walk across the bridge, which even the Rough Guide alleges to be very scary, is undemanding. Scream if you will – but no-one will believe you.

We were treated to a wonderful cameo back at the National Trust tea-room. Two men, probably trained at the Ronnie Barker School of Furniture Removals, arrived in a van to deliver a huge Coca-Cola dispensing machine in a tasteful, fluorescent red frame. It took some time for them to secure this item to a set of wheels. They then manoeuvred it with difficulty down a slope to the tea-room entrance. As Gerard Hoffnung might have put it: unfortunately the outer door did not align with the inner one. By a happy coincidence, the hideous cabinet was of exactly the right dimensions to become wedged decisively between the two door frames. A courteous queue, including

Carrick-a-Rede rope bridge

173

Giant's Causeway, County Antrim

ourselves, formed outside the tea room, while the young man in charge stood helplessly inside, contemplating a lonely struggle for survival relying only on scones, carrot cake and Earl Grey tea. Brute force and a severely bruised door-frame eventually released the prisoner however and all was well. The delivery men took all this phlegmatically – but it was not their finest hour. Did they manage to install the beast? We hoped not. Waiting to find out did not seem like good use of the rest of our day.

This was a quiet weekday in late April. Yet we found the Giant's Causeway under siege from visitors, most of them trying to take photographs of their groups sprawled awkwardly across the basalt pillars. I doubt that anyone can even see the fabric of the Causeway on a busy Bank Holiday. We avoided the shuttle bus and walked along the lovely cliff top past the Causeway, down some steep well engineered steps, then back on a gentle path adorned by outcrops of basalt, to join the crowds. The views stretched away to the Mull of Kintyre and the shadow of Islay. Beyond, and well out of sight, is the tiny storm pitched Isle of Staffa, the next point at which these incredible basalt columns emerge from the sea. Staffa is very isolated. A visit involves a testing journey by small boat from Mull, so numbers are restricted. The huge, endless sea cavern, reached via an adventurous walk across the sea-worn basalt, make it a very special place, worthy of a fine overture. As befits its World Heritage Site status the Causeway is unquestionably magnificent – especially out of hours. But do go to Staffa.

We beetled on to claim a fleeting view of Portrush and Portstewart, the two big resorts with superb blue flag sandy beaches on all sides. Both towns are in the throes of a prolonged building frenzy, with new houses, apartments, bungalows and caravans filling every available nook and cranny. It is fortunate that there is so much beautiful coastline to explore away from these two towns, because their intrinsic appeal is under threat. We learnt later that an exodus of Protestants from Derry to the coast is underway. It is certainly hard to believe that all these new properties could be just for holiday lets.

We headed for Coleraine, alert to the Rough Guide's unusually acerbic comments about its lack of character, expecting the worst. The reality, in warm evening sun with blossom heavy on mature trees fronting elegant houses of a certain age, was enticing. At least a lot of towns in middle England would have to be similarly written off by the RG criteria. Coleraine, as a large, mainly Protestant town which suffered little in the years of violence, wears its good fortune well. The highly contentious decision by Stormont in the late 1960s to develop the second University site here, rather than in Catholic Derry (a city over twice the size) has contributed much to Coleraine's economy and lively culture.

Later we made an initial foray into Derry itself to be sure that we really had established our bearings for the days ahead. The city has a wonderful setting around the broad flow of the River Foyle that opens nearby into its massive Lough. The slope on the west bank is steep. At its crown are the walls of the renowned city fortress built in the early 17th Century by the English to control this most rebellious region of Ireland. The walls are complete, which makes them unique in Ireland and unusual in Europe. The area enclosed is relatively small with a symmetrical road pattern crossing at the diamond, dominated by a handsome sculptured memorial to the fallen of two World Wars. So, yes, we really were in the Six Counties, not the Republic.

INISHOWEN, COUNTY DONEGAL

We crossed the international border by the ferry at the northern end of Lough Foyle. Just short of the terminal stands Magilligan Prison. Once the scene of bitter protests over internment (imprisonment without charge or trial) of suspects in the 1970s, Magilligan is now a civilian prison with a military base attached. Just a frisson of the old tensions touched us as we drove into the high fenced compound to meet the ferry and were thoroughly checked over by a number of uniforms. The borders imposed in the 1921 Partition of Ireland were in many places unmanageable; nowhere more so than on the shores of Lough Foyle. So as we proceeded unsupervised into the Republic on the far bank we reflected how menacing this little crossing must have been a decade or two ago.

Now we had to cope merely with a different currency, distances marked in kilometres, dual language place names and reconfiguration of mobile phone connections. Helmut wondered if we might be driving on the right but Ireland's love affair with the EU does not stretch quite that far.

First halt was Culdaff a tiny settlement with an impressive sweep of golden sand backed by dunes and rocks and at least six visitors. The power of the easterly wind raking across the beach took us by surprise. We beat a path to the shelter of some low rocks which were encrusted in thousands of small mussels and other tidal shellfish – a healthy sign, I presume, of the quality of these waters. To the north west a series of fine cliffs climbed away towards Malin Head, Ireland's most northerly outpost, renowned for its place in the shipping forecast.

The little plantation settlement of Malin itself lies in more sheltered terrain. Like a traditional Anglo-Saxon village in England, Malin's dwellings are neatly aligned around a large, well maintained triangular green. The contrast between this and the customary long street Irish village is striking. Feeling somewhat windblown, we curtailed our researches and crossed to the lone hotel on the green.

Apart from three motor bikers installed outside with their drinks, we had seen little sign of the place being in action. As we walked in, however, we found the place buzzing with trippers and very nearly full. They must all have sneaked in just before we arrived and decided it was good enough for lunch and then afternoon tea as well. It turned out to be one of those magic hostelries that not only provides good food and a warm atmosphere, but also turns the weather around while you eat. The wind eased and the sun came out for us.

FAMINE VILLAGE

Doagh Isle is a remote and wild peninsula in the far north west of the Inishowen headland. We came across yet more stunning beaches to the wild west and around the sheltered inland bay. Our particular interest here was the 'Famine Village' – a highly idiosyncratic enterprise created with passion by a local couple to encourage awareness not just of Irish hardships but of famine as a world wide phenomenon. Some restored original cottages, and some replicas, form a village street. The tour comprises a well researched brew of historical detail and folklore, which Pat, who grew up in here, has lived and absorbed personally. He is a passionate presenter.

The Great Famine struck rural Donegal severely, like much of the west. Its effects were compounded by the 'Great Wind' of January 1839 which had destroyed local fishing boats and overwhelmed some established farms with sandstorms. When the potato crops first failed in 1846 the resources of the community had still not recovered. The first point of escape was Derry, either to find work and settle or to emigrate. Derry prospered in the Famine, as a manufacturing centre, a trading port bringing in American maize and dispatching migrants to the New World. Indeed much of the nine counties of Ulster suffered relatively little. The land inheritance laws here had prevented the subdivision of holdings, and thus a slide into subsistence farming and dependence on the potato.

The emphatic message of the Famine Village endorses what I had learnt in County Clare. Even in the most severe of crop failures, food shortage is rarely the problem. The failure to distribute available food, and to ensure that the hungry can afford it, are the recurrent features of famine then, now and in all sad probability, tomorrow. People succumb to diseases such as typhus and dysentery rather than hunger itself. The rich world outside seems always to be trapped in the same excuses for failing to intervene effectively, including a readiness to blame the victims.

For travellers familiar with the sophisticated presentations and publications common in museums now, the Famine Village will seem different and idiosyncratic –a personal mission, an authentic statement from the heart of Ireland's distant traumas, and a way of making a living in a lonely area. Not to be missed.

REFLECTIONS

The images we carried back from Inishowen were quite conflicting. The expansive beauty and the contrasting seascapes overwhelm. Life is tough here still, especially farming. Poverty may not be as extreme as in the past but it is conspicuous. One in four dwellings in Donegal is either a second home or a holiday let – and occupied seasonally. Tourism, as ever, is a mixed blessing. My imagination cannot shed the impression also of Inishowen as a training ground and an escape route for the paramilitaries, and a transit for arms imports during the 'Troubles'. Its geography makes that all too believable, even inevitable. It now aspires to being a profoundly peaceful place.

Where do Inishowen, and Donegal, belong? We were told that many people feel stronger ties with the six counties of Ulster than with the Republic. Of course Derry has absorbed Donegal families over many generations so that association must be strong. Somehow every small region of Ireland seems to feel separate and distinctive from the rest. History does indeed cast a long shadow.

DUSK

Encouraged by a fine evening we ventured into nearby Banagher Glen, a national wildlife reserve, by way of an ancient, ruined church. Helmut's research had convinced him that some of its holy sand would be ideal to rescue a hapless plant in his garden at home. Neither of us is Catholic so I was able to encourage him fully in this little superstition and even carried the small plastic bottle in support of his villainy. Sadly, whatever sand had once been there had either already been liberated, or just blown away by the winds. The Glen was more rewarding. Heavily wooded, steep and buoyant with the scents of spring, it conjured for us a perfect dusk. The birdsong was strangely muted, even though the air was full of tasty insects. The bats, whirring around us along the track, dined contentedly.

BOY HELMUT

Although we have known each other since our teens, Helmut and I have only incidentally talked about our early years. This was an opportunity to join together the fragments.

Helmut's father, Emil, born in 1904, was the third of thirteen children. He established a successful butcher's shop in Gelsenkirchen which survived Germany's economic and political upheavals up to 1939. Emil's father owned a house comprising four apartments, all occupied by family members, but was financially ruined in the Depression. He therefore sold the house to Emil, the only one with the resources to bail his father out, just before the war. Emil and his wife had their own flat close to the butcher's business. In the war Emil fought in various places, ending up on the Russian Front.

In late 1944 Emil's wife returned from work at the post office to find the flat and the business completely destroyed by a bombing raid. So when Emil was released from the grim Russian transit camp he came back to nothing. The apartment house survived but the sitting tenants, all relatives, refused to accept Emil's claim to the property. So Helmut, their only child, was born in 1946 in his grandmother's three roomed flat. One of these three rooms was sub-let. Work, money and the basics for survival were scarce. Emil was imprisoned for six months by 'the Tommies' for foraging for food in rural north Germany and trading it. He eventually found work at the coal mine. Not until Helmut was about five did they manage to move into a one bedroom apartment in the house Emil owned.

So Helmut had quite a tough start but within a secure family. Like so many Germans, Helmut's parents had been apolitical, intimidated by the Nazi swagger and seeing no alternative to compliance. Now they buckled down to the challenges of re-building their lives from scratch. There were few frills – and no photos from those years.

Helmut quickly flourished at his school, which served a poor, tough community. There was no formal corporal punishment but a lot of casual sadism by teachers – dragging pupils by their hair or pinched flesh to their feet. Only Helmut and one girl from his group progressed to the Gymnasium (Grammar School). More were certainly capable but were uncomfortable at the idea of moving away from the friends and locality they knew best. The selection process involved spending three days of assessment at the Gymnasium. A few years later Helmut was singled out by staff as the ideal candidate for a national scholarship to Atlantic College, an international sixth form college in South Wales. The highly competitive selection process brought together students from across Germany, most of them from much more advantaged circumstances than Helmut and some of them parading an inflated sense of social superiority.

I knew nothing of all this when I first met Helmut but I can only presume some common social heritage enabled us to communicate comfortably. We responded to the egalitarian and idealistic principles on which the college was based. We also reeled at the bewilderingly intensive early weeks, compounded by inevitable homesickness. We soon formed the backbone of a flawless, if eccentric, defence in the college football team.

Helmut came to stay with me at home in January a few days before our first return to AC. My mother, now in her nineties, still remembers with some distress, her feelings at the news that a German boy was coming to stay. Oh not a German please. She had lived in London through both World Wars and wished for no reminders of her enemies. Like Helmut's mother, she had hated seeing her boy disappear to a mysterious castle in South Wales; feelings were still raw. Helmut mended most of that in just a few days. Here was a gentle, quietly spoken but lively and funny young man who was already growing to love Britain. Whatever else Atlantic College did or did not achieve, here was a powerful cameo of reconciliation. I think it was important also for my father who had spent his war in the Metropolitan Police and knew at first hand how much terror and misery the Luftwaffe inflicted night by night on London.

My return visit to stay briefly with Helmut came the following summer. Neither of us can now remember how the four of us managed to organise our sleeping in the little flat. I do recall clearly the generosity of his parents' welcome for me and their pleasure in our friendship. I was there as well in their living room in June 1966 when England won the World Cup. No further comment.

So what had Emil thought about Helmut going off to school in Britain, and then bringing an Englishman to stay? It was the Russians that Emil hated and mistrusted, not the Brits. Even though he had been imprisoned by the Tommies in 1946 he bore no ill-will. Indeed, he was, at 60 when I first met him, fit, strong, lively and generous – without a hint of aggression to anyone. He was, like my own father, simply ambitious for his son to have a better life chances than he had been dealt.

DERRY AND THE BOGSIDE

We had enjoyed the invigorating air of the Antrim and Donegal coasts. Now we were ready to apply ourselves to more weighty matters. Free Derry Tours, a community based initiative, escort groups around the key points of Derry and the Bogside. For us this appealed as an opportunity to steal beyond the authorised version of history and engage in a live dialogue. It turned out to be revealing and challenging. At 11am on Sunday morning the two of us crossed the street below the City Walls to approach the only other person in view. This was Declan, our guide. We two were his group.

This venture was illuminating in two ways. First, the geography made sense of the history. I had read descriptions of Derry and studied maps but only when we stood with Declan overlooking the Bogside from the edge of the city walls did my fragments of understanding connect. A river course used to run to the west of the old city. As it dried out a community grew up on the low ground below the walls. Hence the 'Bog Side'. It was completely rebuilt in the 1970s so some historical imagination is needed. The old community of about twelve thousand lived within a tight maze of terraced streets, with scarcely a breath of air in between them. The new housing, similar to many new build, low cost estates in England, holds less than five thousand. Others were dispersed westward to the Creggan, adjacent and visible atop a substantial hillside.

An extensive steep grass embankment now serves as a visual buffer between the Bogside and the old city walls of Derry. For a century and more the mean terraces climbed to touch these very walls so that the scope for sectarian aggravation across backyards was endless. Viewed from the Bogside, the citadel towers symbolically over the Catholic community. A lofty obelisk surmounted by a statue of George Walker, Protestant hero of the one hundred and five day siege of Derry in 1689, completed a triumphalist skyline. It was blown up in 1973 by the IRA, abetted by sympathetic Welsh miners. Nearby stands the imposing Apprentice Boys Hall, a further expression of the Protestant Ascendancy. The alienation between the two communities could hardly have been more graphic.

The second insight came from Declan himself who openly conveyed an authentic voice from the Bogside community. We were

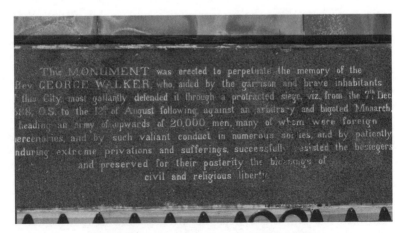

**Derry: monument plaque to George Walker,
hero of siege of Derry 1689, on City Walls above Bogside.
The obelisk was blown up by IRA in 1972**

hearing the story without the spin of politicians or journalists. We counted it a privilege to meet with him. Born in 1969 he was just three when Bloody Sunday split his world asunder. He grew up in the deepest of the crisis that pitched his aggrieved community against the might first of the Protestant authorities, and then of the British forces. He learnt to throw stones, then maybe worse. He had no doubt of the justice of his cause. Now he is proud that his community at last has ownership of its affairs. Growing up on the Bogside is still tough but the grievances are largely overcome. Like thinking folk on all sides, including the Brits, Declan searches for explanations. Why did the agony of attrition last so long? Could the messy compromise not have been achieved sooner and at less cost to all? As often in war, military conflict generated its own justification, however profound the madness became.

Since the Partition of Ireland in 1921 and the creation of two separate states, the Bogside had simmered with resentment at the outrageous sectarian discrimination and exclusion it faced. The situation became tinder-dry with the mutual fears of the two traditions. The disaster of the 1970s was triggered, like so many rebellions, by hopes of better times. The Civil Rights Movement in the USA provided the inspiration here for peaceful mass protest fronted with dignity and passion by Bernadette Devlin (McAliskey). Inevitably the paranoid Ulster authorities were convinced that this was a façade for an IRA-led insurrection. As so often Westminster followed Stormont's lead. Whatever potential existed for a positive negotiation was blown away by the heavy handedness of the RUC. Hope was briefly re-born when the arrival of British troops was welcomed by the Catholic community as offering an even-handed authority.

Then, on 30th January 1972, British paras shot dead thirteen fleeing, unarmed marchers in the Bogside. No soldiers were injured. In 2008, at long last, the Saville Commission is due to report definitively on these events – a decade after it was set up by Tony Blair and thirty six years after the lives were lost. Bloody Sunday signalled the start of a terrible thirty year war and its dreadful atrocities. Britain had trained some of those it now regarded as terrorists. Many Catholics had, for want of other employment, served in HM Forces. So their skills with guns and explosives had been learnt in the army they now confronted.

The politicians now jostle to take credit for making peace. Will any of them ever be persuaded to acknowledge responsibility for keeping the conflict alive for so long? And will they at last concede to the political heroism of John Hume?

The famous murals remain, including the house-end with the iconic 'You are now entering Free Derry'. Republican flags still fly. Their menace has gone but they commemorate a visceral struggle for survival and equality. There are moving, chilling monuments to the victims of Bloody Sunday and to those who died in the 1981 hunger strikes. Sadness is everywhere but the future, gradually, falteringly, looks better.

Declan is a youth worker here, where still nearly fifty per cent sixteen to nineteen year olds are unemployed. He would not have wanted to talk to the likes of me ten, certainly fifteen, years ago. Now

Bogside terraced house end preserved as symbol of community's struggle in 1970s

Republican memorial sculpture c1990

his message is positive. The hatred has given way to a belief and pride in building this community for itself. There has been no liberating Mandela here – though John Hume, leader of the SDLP and the heartbeat of this community came close. He experienced all the grief and bitterness of life in the Bogside but worked unflinchingly for dialogue to resolve the conflict. Now this community needs its heroes at ground level to tackle the hard graft of recovery.

We later visited the extraordinary Free Derry Museum. It has a compelling display of the tortured history of the Bogside, including some original film from 1972. We were escorted by a brother of one of the Bloody Sunday victims, who was rightly interested in our reasons for visiting. Less a museum than a courageous statement from a community emerging into the light. It has just a few publications on sale. Robert Fiske's cogent, powerful speech on the thirtieth anniversary of Bloody Sunday says it all.

You come very close to history here. Whatever your views, this is a chance to hear the authentic voice of a once stricken community. If you visit Northern Ireland, go to Derry and listen to the Bogside.

TO THE LIGHTHOUSE

We needed time to reflect on the intensive and emotional encounter with Declan and, on a warm and sunny Sunday afternoon we, along with too many others, were inevitably drawn to the beach. On the west coast of Lough Foyle we passed a huge crowd, mainly families, gathering for a Gaelic football event. By the lighthouse at Inishowen Head we found some quiet rocks above a beach and settled to watching terns, gannets, shag and gulls perform acrobatics in search of sand eels and fish. Their energetic territorial disputes added to the entertainment. This was Helmut's induction into observing sea-birds. Through binoculars we could see much of the Antrim coast and again the shadow of the Scottish mainland.

Crossing by ferry to Magilligan, we passed another long line of cars, this time attending not football, but a church service. We sought out a very different beach to end the day. This was by the quiet western edge of the Lough, on a huge stretch of sand backed by dunes. I was convinced this would be ideal territory for waders but there was surprisingly little birdlife in evidence. The silver light as the sun dropped behind the Donegal hills was entrancing enough.

THE SPERRIN HILLS

South from Dungiven lies a range of lofty rounded hills which caught our eye from every angle. The Sperrins, a large expanse of upland and valleys, was the domain of prehistoric hunters and settlers. This terrain delighted Helmut and we resolved to claim one of these lonely tops for the German flag. Access is easy enough in that there are few fences. However, such paths as there are tend to cross from valley to valley. So the assault on our chosen summit wandered clumsily through sodden tussocks and peat bog. The views on a hazily sunny morning made up for the spongy terrain. The top of the hill at nearly seven hundred metres cleverly retreated from us behind every peaty terrace.

We took shelter from a growing wind for coffee and biscuits – such hardship. My feet, which are fragile, poor things, declared that their ration of hard work was complete and pointed resolutely downhill now. I conceded. But the German half of the alliance persisted to claim the desolate trig point, re-naming it – fittingly – Cnoc Knut.

I reached the road to be approached by a small, battered white van, the only vehicle for miles. The eighty nine year old occupant had very few teeth and was deaf, a problem not helped by the noisy engine. Our versions of English were also a long way apart so it was a fitful conversation. He wanted me to know that it was his land we had walked on, not so much as a complaint as a point of interest. He observed that I had walked down quite slowly for a youngster – a cunning mixture of insult and flattery. His active farming days are almost gone now and he has no family to take over his land; a familiar story. I asked him how he felt about the future now that the guns had stopped. Well yes it had to be better; but the gist of his response was to call a curse on all their houses. He spat out the phrase 'sectarian politicians' several times. His hero was De Valera – hardly the most accommodating of leaders but one whose stature seems still to loom over all successors. We wished each other well and his vehicle chugged off into the northern valley.

We took a rather circuitous route back, trundling through two more the very distinctive but rather bleak, plantation towns. The very broad avenues are lined by unpretentious rows of small shops and houses. In a few years I am sure these will be bustling with visitor information centres, focusing on the local history and the delights of the Sperrins, with coffee shops to distract weary travellers. As yet though, nothing of the sort. By chance we came across a conference centre which also fed and watered passing strangers. The mansion was located in mature, beautiful woodland. So we found ourselves at a table in an open courtyard which, in the strong afternoon sun, could have been transposed from the Mediterranean. Time for some more searching reflections on what difference Atlantic College had meant to us.

THE CASTLE IN WALES

Atlantic College took both of us from drab urban environments and dropped us into a fairy-tale castle perched on the cliffs in South Wales. We both had difficulties in adjusting to being away from home but the excitement of being in such a place undoubtedly helped the transition. In retrospect the charm of St Donat's gives a dreamlike blur to all the memories. It is easy to forget how much it rained there – not heavy downpours so much as persistent drizzle.

It is also easy to forget how much greater the challenge was for the students whose first language was not English. Helmut's first unnerving encounter occurred at the Globe Inn, in Llantwit Major, on his first journey to the college. As he took his first sip of his beer he found the barman giving him an accusing stare. What was wrong? Too young (in fact yes)? Did they not serve Germans (rarely)? No – in Britain you pay before you drink, in Germany afterwards.

All students at AC were on scholarships – national, local or industrial. I faced too little competition to win my place and arrived, I suspect, a bit by accident. Helmut felt he carried the expectations of Germany on his shoulders. Six of the country's best students had been chosen through an exhaustive process. He found this quite a burden.

From day one we were deliberately kept very busy. Most days began with a fifty metre swim in the open air pool. Lessons ran on six mornings and five evenings each week. Everyone studied at least two languages. Conventional barriers between arts and sciences were discounted. The five afternoons were committed to activities, mainly preparing to run local coastal rescue services. Team games were conceded as extras but the emphasis was on personal development and service, not competition. Cricket, the game of empire, was allowed to feature only on those rare and informal occasions when a few of us managed to persuade the likes of Helmut to field at third man to demonstrate the internationalisation of the game. He seemed strangely resistant to cricket, associating it too easily with falling asleep in the sun and being struck by a leather rock. So Helmut wisely stuck to soccer and played alongside a certain John Toshack for Wales Under 18s.

The college wore its values on its sleeve. It tried to ensure equality of esteem for all who worked or studied there. It expected us to take real responsibility (not the make-believe of prefects). It used competition but did not worship it. It adhered to no religious creed but encouraged voluntary observance. It promoted 'international understanding' without really unpacking what that meant. This was post-war language, which now sounds almost quaint; the notion of multi-cultural education was new (and is now itself worn out). Perhaps there were just too many Brits among both students and staff for the issues to open up effectively. Perhaps it was all meant to happen by osmosis; and happily some of it did.

The student body comprised many who, like the two of us, were quite naïve and impressionable. Others at seventeen, were already streetwise and a bit world weary. They were used to globe trotting and international education. A few were even quite alienated. For Helmut and me the college values made a lasting impact. We never quite understood what the expectations of the founding fathers were for our career destinations. We could not all be ambassadors or politicians. The AC experience should translate well into a thousand career routes. As it happened the peoples of the world came to us in our classrooms and communities. So AC served us well.

It was an energetic, demanding existence at AC, as it should be for seventeen year olds. Of course it had its low points but I never really had any doubts that I had made the best decision. Helmut is more equivocal, for all that it helped him to articulate the beliefs that would shape his future. His school experience in Germany was positive. He might have progressed just as well if he had been excused the weighty expectations of his sponsors.

Our university experiences post-AC were dissimilar. I moved on to a second bout of collegiate life, on which I thrived. Helmut initially returned home to the flat and attended the newly established Bochum University which at the time was one of Germany's major building sites. So until Helmut could move into a hall of residence on campus, he travelled from Gelsenkirchen to Bochum by tram, devoting the 90 minute journeys to reading 18th Century English literature; in all a fairly solitary existence. This contrast probably explains our difference in perspectives on AC. Helmut later moved on to Tubingen, one of the oldest, most renowned of Germany's universities, majoring in English and Philosophy. He completed a doctorate, as was expected in Germany, and became a teacher.

A PREHISTORIC TWILIGHT.

Archaeologists regard the Sperrins region as rich in prehistoric sites but, as a result of farming activities, there is not a great deal left for the layperson to see. The exception is Ballygroll – a 'prehistoric complex' a few miles east of Derry. A single fingerpost from a minor road is the only hint of Ballygroll's existence but the site is well preserved and interpreted. It includes evidence from across two millennia – communal burial cairns, small stone circles, wedge tombs and domestic huts. Beyond are the traces of ancient field patterns as well. The remains are unspectacular but such a configuration in one place is unusual.

The light was fading and the temperature falling as we explored. The nearly full moon, low in the sky just beyond the site, was in direct opposition to the setting sun behind us. We needed a latterday Neolithic mind to interpret the astronomical significance of this, but we contented ourselves with the spectacle. Such light encourages the imagination; on these gentle, overgrown slopes prehistoric settlers made life work for fifty or more generations. That is enough.

THE BEACH AT FAHAN

After a further sweep through Derry to make our last connections and a pause in the excellent the city bookshop, we set off in yet more bright sunshine (apologies if that phrase has become tedious but it somehow, in Ireland, seems worth repeating) into Donegal. Again we crossed the barely visible international boundary. We climbed the serpentine road to Grianan Ailigh. The views are magnificent, taking in almost the whole of Donegal. The intriguing feature that crowns the hill, a restored circular fortress, disguises a long history. It certainly has prehistoric origins, probably a Neolithic burial site. Christian missionaries adopted the hill top and then for centuries it was the royal capital of the O'Neill dynasty. Its secrets are well hidden however. The views win by many a mile.

The three kilometre beach above Fahan on Lough Swilly looked special when we glimpsed it a few days earlier. It now provided a perfect retreat for some slow strolling by (and even in) the gentle sea. We reflected on our week of discovery in the north of Ireland and how we would re-adjust on our returns.

Then we turned our thoughts to the balance sheet for our generation. To the positive: those hard fought social values – equality, respect, fairness – are making a huge difference to ordinary people's lives. Germany's transformation to a stable democracy for six decades, and its collective will to come to terms with its history, are too easily taken for granted. Britain's progress seems muddled by comparison but still represents a transformation. We celebrate our achievements but still become very tangled and argumentative when confronted with the more grisly realities of our past.

We inevitably turned to the deficits. How can it be that, in these open and prosperous societies, our governments still resort so routinely to lies and condescension on the big issues? We too easily rehearsed a few recent examples – Iraq, nuclear power, arms deals, Third World debt, climate change and, close to hand, the dirty collusion in Ireland.

There are always plenty of persuasive excuses for secrecy and double dealing. Do we challenge these hard enough? Is such corrupted democracy the best we can ever achieve?

Solemn thoughts on a beautiful beach; but we were mesmerised by our surroundings. It was a tough call to leave that seashore.

REFLECTIONS AND RETURNS

This was a special and satisfying week. We had experienced a region on the cusp of significant change. The sense of cautious optimism, not least in the Bogside, came across in almost every conversation. The separation of the two communities will continue. There is limited appetite for integration in schooling or housing. Is the new Executive interested in forcing the issue? There is room enough for the two traditions to live apart, with most towns bearing clear allegiance. It might look like apartheid but increasingly the communities enjoy fairly distributed resources and rights. Reports of a Protestant exodus from Derry to the coastal towns are all too plausible. Perhaps after thirty five years of conflict and nearly four thousand deaths it may be time to lie low and hope; and quietly to wonder what it was all for. For the first time since 1921 the boundary seems to have been accepted on all sides; and it seems to have become largely symbolic. We often crossed it without noticing. Will it still seem relevant a generation ahead? Or if the Scots find a way to vote on secession, will some in the six counties not seek a choice too?

We left soon after 6am, in yet more sunshine, for Belfast. We should not have been surprised by the number of many people commuting from Derry to Belfast, or by the extensive roadworks. We parted in high spirits after a rich and stirring week, which had been great fun as well. Helmut's journey proceeded, as his heritage demands, punctually and efficiently. My ferry was held up for three hours for a hydraulics repair. I was keen to be home to receive that latest news from Germany of little Knut.

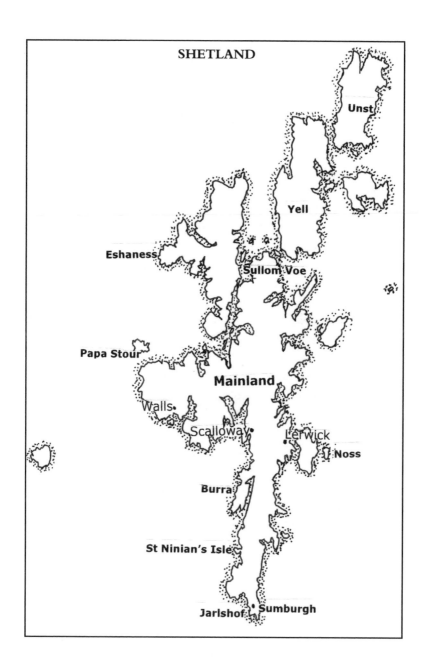

10.   SHETLAND

VIEWED FROM SHETLAND the UK is remote. Edinburgh is seven hundred kilometres away, London thirteen hundred; Bergen in Norway a mere three fifty. It lies further north than Moscow, Stockholm and the southern tip of Greenland. Three seas pound its shores – Atlantic, Norwegian and North. Fifteen of the one hundred islands are home to twenty two thousand people, with just eight thousand in Lerwick, the capital. Taken together these few facts explain much. Self sufficiency, built on nautical skills and a hardy relationship with the land, dominates the core of Shetland's history and character. Shetland is very different.

The adventurer who joined me on this longest journey was Ian, whom I have known since 1969. Ian traversed much of the Scottish Highlands solo in his late teens and is a skilled mountaineer. Like me, he had long conjured an aspiration to reach the Northern Isles. So we travelled with relish, undiminished even when he launched hot coffee into my lap at Tebay. The joy of this week was largely in sharing our mutual enthusiasm for wild landscapes and for working out how life in these distant islands has been sustained.

Just this once we flew in. We would have preferred the twenty four hour ferry from Aberdeen but the costs and extra time involved were prohibitive. The drive north on a storm-lashed M6 offered a symbolic rehearsal for the week. We then tangled with competitive traffic to reach Edinburgh Airport late on a Friday afternoon. The whole project seemed to be at risk when Ian's hand luggage set off the alarms at security. His offensive weapon comprised two plastic bottles, which were duly confiscated.

The flight in a forty seater turbo-prop plane was a treat, taking us over the glorious Forth bridges, Perth and Wick, then east of the Orkneys and within sight of Fair Isle, to the southernmost tip of Shetland at Sumburgh. We were collected by minibus, which proceeded at about the same speed as the plane to a hire car depot. In no time we were enjoying our first experience of Shetland's first-class, nearly empty roads, taking in the green, shapely but treeless landscapes, rarely out of sight of the sea.

Our roost was on Burra, south west of Lerwick, a series of islands joined to Mainland by narrow bridges. Like most dwellings here ours was sturdy, single storey and well maintained – a private house rather than a holiday home. The owner, strikingly Nordic in appearance, had grown up here. Many times we tumbled through the entrance door grateful for the calm warmth of this happy bungalow. Its alignment meant that the narrow path between the door and the outhouse formed a perfect wind tunnel for the incessant westerly winds. An ideal test bed for a domestic wind turbine.

This venture was given an uncanny symmetry by two meetings at the start and finish of the week. The first was with David, collaborator in the Orkney trip over eighteen months before. Prior to that David and I had lost contact for thirty five years. He had been inspired enough by Orkney to persuade Josephine that they really must return to the Northern Isles. Our visits overlapped, coincidentally, by about fifteen hours, so we met in a Lerwick hotel over a late dinner.

It was as well for me that they had enjoyed their week, wild and windy as it had proved. David had prepared his ground effectively. If the trip had been a disaster he would blame me; if a success, then all Brownie points went to him. They had overstocked with beer and wine; his reserves, gifted to us, lasted the week. Their only setback occurred when they misguidedly took a pub poster announcing 'Live Music on Wednesdays' at face value. They walked into an almost empty and eerily silent hostelry that could have been a Hitchcock film set. A lone drinker, possibly an ancient mariner, was summoned by his muse to demand accusingly: 'What brings you two in here then?' David pointed to the poster but he can spot a lost cause when he sees one. Truth be told, they had found Lerwick much less engaging than Kirkwall. We drove back to Burra in an apparently endless twilight, still collecting our initial impressions of the vast landscapes and tiny settlements.

THE GOVERNOR

Ian retired a few years ago as a creative, successful secondary Headteacher.

His sharpness of wit, easy efficiency and energy remain much as they were when I first knew him. Annoyingly, so does his weight and physique. He has great generosity of spirit, endless ingenuity as a problem solver and an unusual ability to challenge rigorously without causing offence. A week with Ian would be eventful even if we were treated to relentless force nine winds and rain. I adopted the cunning tactic of letting him think he was in charge of our adventures. He countered with servility, like a latter-day Jeeves, rising early to prepare cooked breakfasts and packed lunches. He even volunteered for the bunk, leaving the double bed to his taller, heavier team member. I conceded with gratitude, not even complaining at having to sleep diagonally.

Long ago when we were humble teachers together in a large, busy comprehensive school, Ian recruited me to help him run the Duke of Edinburgh expeditions. At his instigation I started a training programme in mountain leadership, a terrific experience conducted mainly in the Welsh hills. In reality I learnt as much from Ian as from the award, although the course of true mountaineering did not always run smooth.

Most memorable was a D of E trial weekend in the Black Mountains near Crickhowell. We had gathered so many bronze, silver and gold candidates that every tent the school owned – and some that it didn't – were called into action. The base camp was flat and sheltered alongside the river in the forest, so we had few worries. On the second evening Ian and I set out to check that the students camping away from the base were safe and in good shape. One group had shown initiative by moving from their agreed location to find better shelter from gathering winds. It was fully dark when our torches found them behind a haystack in a field with a thousand eyes – sheep.

It was about 10pm when we returned to the base to be greeted by voices shouting that Patsy had fallen in the stream and hurt her ankle. If anyone was going to fall in the stream it would have to be Patsy, delightful student though she was. The women staff had delayed a decision about taking her to hospital until Ian returned. The injury clearly needed an X-ray so Ian set off on the 40 mile round trip to hospital, with Patsy stretched out in the minibus. (In 2007, of course, such a journey would require a female teacher present, but the 1970s were still such innocent days).

At the base camp we settled everyone else down in their tents. The winds through the forest had gathered strength and it was raining heavily. The two staff tents, adjacent to each other in the circle, were the oldest A-frame items from the dusty back shelf of the camp store at school. Ian returned at 2pm with a duly plastered Patsy and joined me in the veteran tent. About twenty minutes later a terrific gust of wind spun through the site, simultaneously snapping one of the A poles in both of the staff tents. I was grovelling between the collapsed canvas and detritus of our belongings, vaguely planning a retreat to the minibus and hoping the pupils' tents had survived. Ian, with great presence of mind for someone who had enjoyed all of ten minutes' sleep, sprang into action. He rescued the two intact poles and re-instated one tent for the four of us, packed sardine style for the rest of the night.

My first recollections on waking were of many shocked little voices, chattering across the site. 'They didn't' 'They weren't' 'What all four of them'….'Ooooh, that's a good one'….'What if we'd done that?' and so on. Then giggles and laughter. No mobile 'phones to ring the Sun with lurid stories and photos. Nor the learned malice that now afflicts some pupils' attitudes towards teachers. Not even a reprimand as the news spread back at school next week. So this infamous weekend passed innocently into the legend of the school and we two plotted the next opportunity to dice with misfortune.

I learnt a lot from Ian.

TWO CAPITALS, ELEVEN POOLS AND A BUS

We had, with our beloved maps and guidebooks, planned plenty of ambitious little expeditions in advance and now waited upon the weather to determine which would be feasible. Day One however was easy. We would start in Lerwick come what may. And what came was a force eight – not flattering to Lerwick, a town that needs all the help it can get to lighten a stolid and rather forbidding aspect. Its character grew on us over the week, especially as we discovered the lines of the old harbour, now concealed by later building. The isle of Bressay protects the port comprehensively from the worst of the elements. What a haven it must be for trawlers retreating before Atlantic storms.

The modern quay is extensive. At the northern end are the trawler docks, the huge fish processing plants with other industrial units. The ferry from Aberdeen docks in the central section alongside other passenger services. Next is the harbour for the Lifeboat, smaller craft and visiting ships. 'Arctic Sunrise', the Greenpeace ship in northern waters, campaigning to protect cod stocks and to curtail whaling, was in town. The other mooring was occupied by a large HM Customs vessel, possibly heading to the same waters as Greenpeace.

One evening we explored at dusk (it never really grew fully dark) along Commercial Street, the line of the ancient quay. The houses to seaward bear the convincing character of fishermen's hideouts and smugglers' dens from the past. Lerwick is a functional workaday place, with too much serious business and weather to be bothered with architectural frills. But the atmosphere of the old quay area conjures images of mistier, shadier dealings when battles for trade were fought in earnest and common cause was made to deceive the Customs men.

Later in the week an impressive fifty year old Swedish ship, the Stockholm, docked. We stole a conversation with the amiable captain as he came ashore. His ship had started life as a lighthouse supply vessel, rendered redundant by automation. Its superb condition belied the tough life it must have endured. The beautifully timbered bridge, high quality deck fittings and fine lines disguised the reality of a very heavy duty vessel. It now takes expedition- class tourists to the Arctic north of Scandinavia. We were tempted to stow away.

We tacked skilfully along the Lerwick shoreline, taking necessary shelter in the Tourist Office and the wonderful Shetland Times bookshop. Its local and maritime coverage is excellent and, despite the limited space, the provision in most categories would put many city bookshops to shame. Ian and I were, however, resolute in resisting significant expenditure. I did, as usual, invest in a copy of the weekly local paper, in this case the Shetland Times. For a town of under eight thousand and island-wide communities of another fourteen thousand, the paper is of remarkable quality. First it is very well written, with headlines that avoid the hackneyed wordplay so drearily predictable across most of the UK's regional press. Secondly its perspectives on politics, the maritime economy and Shetland's relations with its neighbours are thoughtful and well crafted. Its format is traditional but at least it has not thrown out substance in pursuit of style and celebrity. Worth much more than 70p.

We also needed supplies. Jeeves had spent some of the early hours plotting menus and necessary purchases down to a fine line. His shopping lists are models of detail and restraint, with proportions measured and little risk of waste. His only extravagance was a large personal supply of Kit-Kats. I have rarely experienced such discipline when raiding a supermarket. Lerwick boasts two good sized stores, largely indistinguishable from most other UK supermarkets. Both places seemed busy. Checkout queues were slow. How do eight thousand people manage to make two such shops appear crowded? Do they pay people to buy supplies from one place and trade them in at the other, just to keep the turnover figures high?

Shetland's other capital is Scalloway. It was stripped of its birthright in 1708 as result of some complex dirty deeds involving trade wars between the Dutch and the French. Until then Lerwick had been just another of the hundred small fishing villages around the shores of Shetland.

Scalloway: ancient capital of Shetland, well sheltered from Atlantic by string of islands

We had been puzzled as to how Scalloway could have been the historic capital. It faces the wild Atlantic and is on the far side of Mainland for Viking longships crossing to and from Norway. We soon realised that Scalloway is very well protected from westerly storms by a constellation of small islands and has an accessible deep water harbour. It now has less than one thousand inhabitants (at least until the newly built houses are occupied). Like Stromness, on Orkney, which suffered a similar relegation at the hands of Kirkwall, Scalloway wears its decline rather heavily. The dominant castle and the harbour itself tell of a more significant era. The two towns are less than five miles apart, joined by tortuous hilly roads, alongside which stands (or perhaps leans) Shetland's major golf course. A fine, challenging, destination for the next Ryder Cup. Of course land routes scarcely mattered until the last century; the sea and the harbours provided the crucial links.

The roads on most of Shetland are of magnificent quality, well engineered and maintained. Like the finest mountain roads elsewhere in the UK – into Glen Coe or Telford's routeway through Snowdonia – Shetland's highways also manage somehow to add to the grandeur and scale of the terrain. The appearance of the sea at every turn, ahead and to either side enhances the sense of floating through the landscape. And they are so unbelievably empty. A marvellous place to take a driving test – although of limited value if you move to Glasgow.

Tiny Scalloway has a swimming pool and leisure centre that would do credit to a fair-sized English town. Shetland has eleven public pools – one per two thousand people. This has come about from the islands' share of the oil revenues. Investment in the infrastructure of roads, bridges, schools, port development, ferries and leisure facilities has been extensive and creates a striking sense of well-being in these communities. It has made life in a tough environment more manageable and enjoyable. By stages we concluded that Shetland conveys much more the feel and appearance of Scandinavia than of mainland Scotland.

Scalloway also recalls an heroic episode in Shetland's history. When Norway fell to the Nazis in 1940 it was left with few lines of communication to the wider world. A courageous Resistance to the Nazis and the Quisling regime within the country was supported in Shetland by a special unit, about one hundred strong and including many local trawlermen. The unit's base was initially at Lunna House, a remote mansion in the north-west of Mainland. Then it was moved to Scalloway. The Norway Bus, as it was known, operated in extreme secrecy and at high risk but with considerable success, carrying out sabotage missions, delivering arms and materials, dispatching and rescuing Norwegian agents. Without the specialist knowledge and skills of Shetland skippers such resistance activities would have been unsustainable. The collaboration between Shetland and Norway is still celebrated by re-unions and ceremonials. Scalloway itself has a striking monument constructed of stone from each of the linked settlements in Norway.

A small museum in Scalloway commemorates the Norway Bus. We escaped into it from the teeth of the westerly gale, raging against the seafront. This venture is a charity run by volunteers. The ageing displays tell the story well. However, in light of the splendid new Shetland Museum in Lerwick, to be opened by Charles, Camilla and Queen Sonja of Norway, just a few days after our trip, let's hope the Scalloway museum is given a makeover soon. It records a noble, sustained undertaking that required individual courage and a steady nerve from the community that nurtured the Norway Bus. That

Co-ordination for acts of sabotage depended on well established radio communications. The SHETLAND BUS took over about sixty radio transmitters along with operators and saboteurs.

Some of the acts of sabotage successfully carried out :-
Sabotage of ships in OSLO
Blowing-up of JØRSTAD railway bridge in SNÅSNA.
Sabotage of anti-aircraft shells at RJUKAN.
Hi-jacking of all tugs in FREDRIKSTAD harbour. These were sailed to a SWEDISH port.
Fighting between resistance units and German troops.
Sabotage of tank installations at SON and SVELVIK.
Blowing-up of machines and guns at KONGSBERG and
Blowing-up of BAERUG railway bridge.
Blowing-up of the headquarters of the GERMAN controlled state police in OSLO.
Sinking of the DONAU "slave ship"
Sabotaging the floating crane at MOSS, "NORSK ALUMINIUM." "PERKURE," and the ' SKF ' ball-bearing factory

The Norway Shetland Bus: record of actions undertaken by Shetlanders on behalf of Norway's resistance to the Nazis

generation is fading now. Its efforts deserve due recognition and to be an important marker for all of Shetland's visitors.

THE BURRA PENINSULAS

We left urban Shetland to explore some wild headlands south of Scalloway. The sun made an appearance in the mid-afternoon but the wind yielded not at all. The sea to the west was by now deeply angry and throwing monstrous waves at cliffs and beaches. We dropped down to a magnificent crescent shaped causeway, picking our way along the beach. A sad tiny lamb pleaded with us for help. It must have been the last of the litter, too weak to stand much chance of survival and so abandoned by the ewe. I lifted it —weighing less than nothing – back over the fence where the rest of its tribe were making the usual sheeply fuss; but no ewe responded. Later we left a message for the croft.

Abandoned, sickly lamb

Sheep shelter (Burra)

To every side there were signs of long abandoned settlements. An historical society is restoring one set of these with splendid new thatch and heavy stone walls, immaculately whitewashed, presumably for exhibition to the public before long. Two unpretentious constructions caught our eye. A single storey prefabricated cabin, perhaps liberated and transported from an early holiday camp, stood sentinel at the end of the causeway. Its survival in such a location seemed improbable despite signs of occupation, perhaps as a crofter's shelter. A short distance further was the hull of an upturned boat, converted to a shelter, with breeze-block walls and encrusted with shells. This would be the better bet in a storm but was evidently reserved for the sheep. Suddenly, from behind the boat-roofed refuge a large brown bird took wing. Our first Great Skua of the trip, and not immediately recognised.

Trusting to our OS map we made for a sea arch along the cliffs, beating into the wild winds. Just below our path, on sloping rocks, was an arctic tern colony, which predictably went into a fearful frenzy as we trespassed. They are such beautiful acrobatic birds, slight of frame, with slender tail streamers and always hyperactive. Whether plunging repeatedly just below the surface of the sea for eels or fish, or wheeling with collective menace about the heads of alien intruders, they seem over-excited, using up disproportionate amounts of energy to limited effect. Most of their extravagant dives – wonderful to watch – produce no catch and their attacks on humans also fall short; perhaps we looked too old and tough to be shredded for the chicks.

The sea arch – still where the OS map had put it – was being furiously attacked by sheets of white water. It was no place for a conversation or to lose your footing. We were now poised above a full westerly horizon. The boiling sea, churning around every resistant outcrop of rocks and pitching spume high into the air, is routine for Shetland, exhilarating for us. What must a force ten be like?

Arctic terns protecting their colony against human intrusion

We took respite in the calm of our house and chanced upon the late stages of the English Cup Final. The early evening sunshine drew us out again and we found another, smaller beach nearby just a few hundred yards from the road. This one even has a car park and well maintained toilets, which we assume means that on warm weekends – now that had us guessing – this is a honeypot for visitors. It deserves to be. The curving golden sands, backed by low cliffs, and edged by steep rocks, look idyllic. We weather beaten two had the place to ourselves for an hour; even the birds seemed to have wearied of the winds that day. Presumably, with twenty hours of daylight they can afford to rest when the weather is particularly hostile.

So our introductions to Shetland were complete. We had sampled enough to shake out our expectations. We realised already that these are landscapes, seascapes and atmosphere to absorb slowly. We wanted to explore different parts of the islands but were determined not to rush around ticking off destinations on a checklist. What is it like to live amidst such powerful winds and seas all the time? The landscapes vary from pastoral to rugged, and although there is endless green to soothe the eye, the lack of trees was, for us, disturbing. To find the sea on all sides so much of the time is a visual delight but even when it settles for an hour or two, the sense of menace is potent.

TRACES OF PRE-HISTORY

The first Neolithic settlers on Shetland probably progressed from the Scottish mainland. Orkney is visible from the north Scottish coast, Fair Isle is just visible from Orkney and the Shetlands can easily be seen from Fair Isle. The Neolithic settlers did not cast as spectacular an imprint here as on Orkney but their presence was extensive and distinctive. We focused on just two major locations, one on West Mainland, a site visited by very few, the other at the southernmost tip of Shetland, visited by every tourist.

Stanydale is located near Walls, on West Mainland. It dates from 2,500BC and was abandoned around 1600BC, by which time the climate had changed significantly for the worse. It is recorded on maps and books as a temple – probably in error. The 'Historic Scotland' roadside finger post exaggerates the distance, which is just a mile of very boggy, now unproductive, moorland. The reward is a site unique in the UK. It is heel shaped, about eight metres by twenty, with grass topped walls standing over one metre high. The edges comprise a series of stone alcoves that were certainly used as domestic dwellings. Two holes in the floor are thought to have held spruce (presumably imported) posts supporting a roof above head height. So by Neolithic standards this was major building enterprise and it does not conform to patterns elsewhere – no burials, no stone circles (although to our untutored eyes a partial circle of sorts could just be imagined 30 metres or so around the site). Climate at the time would have been quite favourable and there is evidence of crop production and field boundaries in the surrounds.

So, on limited evidence, we have a secluded community that created an unusual, well protected settlement for itself, growing crops and rearing livestock. Too easy, I am afraid. First, whoever chose the site must have worked hard to find a location in Shetland from which the sea could not be seen in any direction. Why so? Perhaps the cascading seas here were too much of a threat to dwellings and farmland. Secondly, within a three kilometre radius there are a whole series of Neolithic hut circles and settlements of apparently conventional design, notably the Scord of Broster. Stanydale is not as isolated as it looks. Thirdly, why choose a site so far from fresh and sea water if its sole purpose was to be an ordinary settlement, bent on mere survival?

Stanydale must surely have been a significant location for the settlers in the vicinity. Was it a gathering place as well as a village? Might it have been a royal or priestly community that was serviced by the other settlements? It makes little sense as a defensive site as it is overlooked on two sides. Anyway there is little to suggest that Neolithic settlers engaged in much aggressive rivalry, unlike later, more congested and more organised tribal groupings. So maybe it did serve as a temple after all. But the archaeological evidence is lacking for this and the usual astronomical alignments are either missing or just so sophisticated as to be indecipherable. We tend to look around us at the land and the sea to explain location and purpose. Maybe Stanydale was chosen partly because of its untroubled view to the life-governing heavens. Stanydale is intriguing.

Ian and I returned through the quagmires wrestling with such questions. These people were our intellectual equals and could rely on the accumulated practical wisdom of many generations living in the same area. We depend on received technologies and written instructions. They must have been supreme problem solvers just to reach Shetland and to make their society work. Our imaginations cannot take us there but it is worthwhile to keep trying.

Our second diversion into prehistory was in southernmost Shetland. The site bears the imaginative title of Jarlshof, invented by Sir Walter Scott in his novel 'The Pirate'. Cleverly evocative as the name is, it seems a pity that Historic Scotland cannot research an earlier, more authentic version. The Norse settlers themselves must have designated it somehow. Skara Brae on Orkney was buried in dunes for over four millenia; Jarlshof disappeared into the sands for less than two hundred years. At a first viewing it does not compare with Skara Brae, whose unusual intimacy reveals the lives of those last families in their final moments of occupation. But Jarlsof is special in a different way. It demonstrates intricate layers of settlement over four thousand years.

Our impressions of Jarlshof were enhanced by a bright, cold morning and by the privilege of having the site to ourselves. I usually prefer to view sites with just a written guide but here we chose to take the recorded commentary – a wise choice. We were entranced by the beautiful Shetland voice- the tone authoritative, the enunciation perfect, the pitch engaging and the accent as pure as our language allows. We were steered intelligently around the site and spared, by a menu of choices, superfluous dramatic reconstructions. Congratulations to all concerned.

There is little tangible evidence of the Neolithic settlers here because their Bronze Age successors re-used their foundations. Like Skara Brae the site now perches perilously close to the shoreline but the erosion by rising sea levels did not force settlers to abandon Jarlshof. There remains a series of modest Bronze Age hut circles rich in household artefacts and middens containing fragments of shellfish and sea birds. The adjacent Iron Age wheel houses – four circular communal dwellings constructed in stone to well above head height – are both impressive and unusual. They have been partly lost to the sea. After this Pictish settlers occupied the site, with little obvious impact, conveying it for reasons unknown to a family from south west Norway in about 800AD.

The Norse settlers left a significant impact on the site over 400 years, although little more than foundations remain. Their village grew immediately to the landward side of the earlier dwellings. It is striking that the Norse buildings, in contrast to their precursors, are almost all rectangular, with a longhouse that was in use throughout the occupation. The cottages and barns were reconfigured generation by generation. This is by far the most impressive Norse settlement site I have come across on these journeys. As at Skara Brae it was not difficult for our imaginations to populate the wide sweep of the sheltered bay with longboats. Surely they must have had a vernacular name for the place.

The final layer of the Jarlshof story began in the 13th Century with a substantial farm and barn built over part of the Bronze Age site. These buildings were modified frequently before their partial destruction and eventual abandonment in the 17th Century. In the following century most of the site was inundated by 'a great sandblow'; and at the end of the 19th Century a further massive storm breached the dunes revealing enough of the ruins to attract the archaeologists.

We chatted to the custodian wondering if the site was always as empty of visitors as today. Our well meaning question opened another saga. Until late June a trickle of visitors quietly absorb this complicated historical puzzle. Then come the cruise ships, about fifty per season, each offloading a fleet of coaches from Lerwick, each timed to press seventy people through the site in half an hour or less. At least this means Jarlshof balances its books. We drove away anxiously eyeing the horizon for a speeding coach, grateful to have seen this special place in solitude and to have learnt much from it.

Above all go to Skara Brae; but then head for Jarlshof. They make sense together.

ALL THE TALENTS

Ian was born just before the war. He is very proud of the secure, loving and enabling upbringing his parents gave him in the West Riding. His father, born in 1907, was the son of a miner and one of large family.

He made a career in the WR Police in Morley and then in Huddersfield as a CID sergeant — a curious parallel with my father who left rural labour in Berkshire to join the Metropolitan Police. Ian's mother, daughter of a small, and class conscious, businessman, had to give up her work as a secretary when his father joined the Police (around 1930). Both were intelligent and energetic characters, part of a generation that was, to our continuing sadness, denied the educational opportunities it deserved.

Ian was a wiry boy endowed with the sharp wits and vigour of his parents. He quickly became a voracious reader immersing himself in story comics, westerns and fiction. Praise be for public libraries. He also learnt to handle the challenges of playground rivalries, often arriving home with a few cuts and bruises. The teachers too resorted frequently to physical punishment. Ian recalls being caught out poking his fairly harmless pocket knife into his best friend, as boys will. It was a play incident not a fight. However Ian took off at speed to escape the head, a stern, blue suited woman, of short and stocky build. Lacking other options he jumped into an empty dustbin and waited for silence to descend. Unfortunately he lifted the lid an inch to see if further escape was possible just as the formidable lady turned the corner. He suspects that she quite enjoyed inflicting the inevitable caning. Ian's academic qualities and his sporting prowess carried him through such little disasters.

At Queen Elizabeth Grammar School (QEGS) Ian thrived. Bullying on the school bus proved an early aggravation. In the end he landed a decisive punch on the face of the worst perpetrator and was spared any more of his attentions. He took a fleet of 'O' levels at fifteen, although it was only in the sixth form that his enthusiasms and real potential were fired. An inspirational Head of History, Ronald Coleman, who was also in charge of the 'Modern' segment of the Sixth Form, and an imaginative Head of Geography made a significant impression. Ian won a Geography scholarship at Cambridge. Then his father, just forty six and a primary school caretaker, was stricken with a brain tumour. Although he was entitled to a full grant, Ian would not have been able to go to Cambridge had his father died or been disabled; he would have to find work to support the family.

Happily his father recovered. Ian enjoyed Cambridge life to the full, not least in gaining his pilot's licence through the University Air Squadron. As a very promising cricketer Ian was offered a University trial. He missed the event however when a canoeing expedition went badly wrong. The two students set off from Sleaford and beached in the middle of the Wash as the tide fell, re-floating as it rose; but they struck an old sea wall around midnight at the entrance to King's Lynn harbour ripping the base from the canoes. They swam and then waded across the marshes, shredding their feet. An everyday episode in the life of an undergraduate.

Three years was enough. Ian's imagination and ambition had been lit by the prospect of becoming a district officer with the Colonial Service in the Gilbert and Ellice Islands. Some hurdles had first to be overcome. Two years National Service followed as education officer at a joint USAF/ RAF station in Norfolk, home to the THOR missile range, with hotlines to the PM and President. The time proved enjoyable although Ian's hopes of flying were thwarted. Unless he signed on for five years the RAF, reasonably enough, would not offer him a commission and invest in training him. However he did undertake the survival training regime. Ian organised the station's rugby and cricket, ran the film club and the Station magazine – 'the Rocket'.

Then he spent a year at Oxford sharing the training for the Western Pacific High Commission with Glynne, an Irish colleague. They were expected to travel regularly to London for tuition in Gilbertese at the Colonial Office with Miss Paleman, a strict and demanding ex-missionary schoolteacher. No student dare fail the course, which concluded with a photo-shoot of the tutor and 'her boys' outside Westminster Abbey. Glynne made a habit of just missing the train so Ian often endured the two hour exchanges alone, becoming quite proficient. He also fitted in a diploma in Social Anthropology for his own interest. Sadly, Ian and Glynne, after all this training, were advised that, after all, no vacancies existed in the Gilberts. It was the Solomon Islands instead.

The role was very demanding and fulfilling, offering direct responsibility and independent authority way beyond anything a twenty five year old might have expected in the UK. Ian still talks of those five years with excitement and relish. He had not, however, seen clearly enough all that it would demand of him. He and Jane, a couple since schooldays, married after Cambridge. Their two children were born at the local hospital, an ex-American Army Nissen hut complex on Guadalcanal. In an equatorial environment with ninety per cent humidity year round, caring for the health and well-being of two young children was tough. The options that emerged were to send the children back to residential education England, or for Jane to return with them, Ian joining his family for a few months every two years, or for all four to go back. It was no choice at all.

One piece of this jigsaw Ian and I had never discussed was his decision, post Solomons, to go into teaching. He was brilliant at the job, so to me, as a rookie teacher watching for quality performers to emulate, it was immediately obvious why he was doing it. Was it a pragmatic or incidental decision? Far from it. Ian had long conjured another ambition – to be a Head of Sixth Form like his mentor at QEGS. Characteristically Ian never looked back; he relished life in school and, sure enough, was promoted to the role he really wanted and made it his own. Ian's mental and physical attributes would have equipped him to be an RAF pilot, maybe even a county cricketer (so long as he gave up the canoeing), a District Officer or much else. But his generosity of spirit and enthusiasm to see others succeed made him an exceptional teacher and school leader.

I learnt a lot from Ian.

BIRD CITY

It is difficult to find words that capture our delight in the half day boat trip from Lerwick around the islands of Bressay and Noss. It was in all ways superb. The vessel is purpose built with good quality inside shelter, a well-shielded open deck and even a couple of crow's nest seats above for the best views of all. Passenger numbers are restricted to ten allowing for freedom of movement and easy access to quiz the crew. The skipper delivered an authentic commentary with measured wit. He must really love this job to find such a fresh enthusiasm for every trip. His boatmanship was marvellous – and well tested. He could not disguise his disdain for the bureaucracy that surrounds sea-going activities now. As an ex-trawlerman who spent much of his life battling the elements in the most dangerous working environment of all, he found it difficult to take seriously regulation from John Prescott, a sometime steward on liners, and from land-based HSE advisers. He made good play of it all.

We started with an exploration of Lerwick harbour itself. Even as we boarded the boat two red-throated divers displayed their silky skills close by. The star turn was a pod of huge grey seals, a gentlemen's club, which lives off the rich debris of the fish processing industry along Lerwick's north shoreline. In the wild these creatures could never survive so long; in voluntary captivity they face few threats. They closed on our boat certain that some tasty off cuts would come their way from the crewman's bucket.

At the same time some other scavengers joined the boat. Great Skuas – who featured prominently in our week on Shetland – accompanied us on the whole trip, flying very close as we moved and resting on the sea, like benign ducks on a lake, when we stopped. We saw the full range of Skua behaviour on this circuit. For all their acrobatic elegance in flight and their beautiful markings they are cunning, vicious bullies dedicated to pilfering and mugging other birds. We watched a gannet surfacing from a deep dive with fish in its gullet. Two skuas leapt in to stop it taking off. The gannet tried repeatedly to escape their attentions, going below the surface when one skua bit on to a wing tip. By some miracle the gannet managed to take flight and the mobsters looked around for another less seasoned victim.

Later, below the huge cliffs at Noss the skipper was puzzled that so many gannets seemed to have risen en masse and were circling, making an unholy din. He twisted the boat around in the wild water until he spotted the cause of the disturbance. Two skuas appeared to be in mortal combat with each other over some ill-gotten spoils. The rest of bird city was, like a crowd at the Colosseum, urging them on, thrilling to the spectacle of their own arch-enemies at each others' throats.

The skipper waxed eloquent about his favourite sea bird – the guillemot. It has all the skills. It can dive shallow or deep, swim and manoeuvre at extraordinary speed, fly powerfully, land perfectly and it

**Noss Gannets take to the air to observe and celebrate a fight
between two Great Skuas**

offers no obvious threat to other birds. We observed vast colonies of
guillemots, razorbills, and kittiwakes on the first of the towering 150m
plus cliffs. The numbers seemed excessive. The mysterious hierarchies
of bird-world determined that the lowest in the pecking order were
forced to occupy ledges vulnerable to leaping waves.

I was intrigued that the populations seemed to be close to their
limits. The word was that recent breeding seasons had been poor
because of the shortage of sand eels on which the surface feeding birds
depend. The crewman's observations interested me. One idea now is
that the sand eels have not been in short supply but are being driven
deeper because surface temperatures are rising as a result of global
warming; others remain convinced that the eel shoals really have
moved north or east. During this conversation I caught sight of a shag
hurtling low over the water with a lengthy, still struggling eel in its bill;
life looks good for the deep divers.

The next suburb in bird city belonged to the gannets whose colonies
tend to be exclusive. This breeding ground must be on a scale with Bass
Rock and Ailsa Craig. They are wonderful birds, strikingly white in flight

with black wing tips and a pale yellow neck. Their flight is powerful and joyous, their capacity to dive deep from a great height never ceases to excite. They also display so affectionately and artistically on their nests, their necks twisting upwards in mutual regard. I suppose they too have some bad habits but they do not deserve cowardly attacks by skuas.

Ian and I were happily absorbed in this whole, glorious spectacle. He recalled journeys around the Solomons in boats of this size and speed but was also spellbound by the antics of the nesting birds. Our own safety was put at risk by a cheery but rather manic Norwegian with several cameras and lenses who skidded around the deck at high speed, desperate not to miss the best close ups; in so doing he skittled other passengers as they focused on the sea or the teeming sky. We wondered just how many images anyone needs of skuas, who hung almost motionless around the rim of the boat, or of gannets whose collective mass at times darkened the sky.

The afternoon gradually turned from an ominous grey to bright sunshine as we travelled. What more could we ask for? The skipper cast his very expensive submersible camera into sheltered waters while we gathered around two screens on deck. His intimate knowledge of the sea bed made for compelling viewing. He focused on urchins and corals before sweeping through a kelp forest. At once I understood a little more of the kelp harvesting that had for fifty years around 1800 been a crucial earner for the crofters of Harris and Lewis. Kelp is a tall, dark broadleaved seaweed which colonises large areas of the sea bed, its head floating at or near the surface. Once burnt as an ingredient in glass making and soap, it is now making a fashionable return as an iodine-rich health supplement.

We paused in the narrow run of water between Bressay and Noss for another extraordinary tale. Norse records are clear that a causeway still joined these two islands in 1100 – a span of about one hundred metres. By the 16th Century the causeway had completely disappeared. This was not the result of gradual erosion but a massive inundation. Shetland's post ice age history features several tsunami as sea levels rose all around the islands. It seems likely that a smaller scale event occurred in the late middle ages scouring away the land bridge between these two islands, and much else besides.

The skipper checked on everyone's health and proceeded to

indulge in 'a little bit of fun'. He headed the boat at full power into the wilder waters to the south of Bressay giving us a feel for the constant battle that besets Shetland. It was a magnificent, pounding conclusion to a quite magical journey. We wandered the quayside afterwards just collecting our thoughts and relishing a matchless afternoon at sea.

Later we returned to our local shores in pursuit of the perfect sunset. The terns, still seeing us as strangers despite our frequent visits, mounted their frenzied rearguard action, swooping around Ian's head. He now had little fear for a flock of mere terns that might be messy but did not rank in menace with skuas. We retreated just in time to spot a group of grey seals, older male, younger males and females rolling around a few feet away on the stony beach. They promptly took off into the sea – as surprised as we were.

SUMBURGH HEAD AND ST NINIAN'S ISLE

The next afternoon we made time for a slow exploration of the southern tip of Shetland. The RSPB own the headland that teems with kittiwakes, guillemots and, especially, puffins. To all sides, behind every grassy tuft, in every sandy tunnel were puffins – basking, shuffling, preening, posing, greeting each other and just occasionally levering themselves awkwardly into the air to find food for the nestlings. In flight they move at speed with rapid wing beat and are wonderful underwater swimmers. Landing is but a controlled accident. These creatures are designed to live at sea; ten weeks on shore to breed is just a necessary, uncomfortable interlude. Their clownish appearance and behaviour are difficult to resist and a photographer's dream. Nowhere better than Sumburgh.

The headland rises steeply away from the bay with the airport on one side and Jarlshof on the other. It is capped by yet another imposing lighthouse (1819) by Robert Stephenson. Sumburgh must have been a desperate place for shipping prior to that. We were struck, though, by the sadly neglected state of the outbuildings adjoining the light itself. Of course it is automated so no-one lives on site but the decay is seeping deep into the fabric, with windows decaying, masonry exposed to the elements and rust seizing hold of the gangways. No

Sumburgh puffins

doubt all will have been repaired by the time of writing, but not a minute too soon if so.

We met here two of the passengers from the Noss boat trip – happily not the frantic Norwegian cameraman, but a young couple relishing every minute of their time on Shetland, and travelling by public transport. We were to see them twice more. Tourists are spread thinly here – at least until the cruise ships arrive. On the hill top behind the lighthouse stands a cluster of large globes and discs, very much in Bristol fashion. This telecommunications outpost includes one of the UK's few fixed points for the GPS (Global Positioning Satellite) systems on which shipping and mountaineers increasingly rely.

We scanned the map and guides for a further destination on this southern peninsula. It had to be St Ninian's Isle, attached by the slimmest of threads to the west coast. This feature is confidently declared to be the finest tombolo in Europe. The curves of the shell sand causeway are perfectly proportioned. It is a wonderfully picturesque location, dramatically enhanced as the sun lowered through the late afternoon sky. The low cliffs and off-isles stood green

Slender Tombolo joining St Ninian's Isle to mainland.

and shimmering while the backlit mainland was sharp in every detail. We watched a farmer completing some inch perfect ploughing, supervised and advised by his attentive sheepdog. Common gulls from half of Shetland had descended to gather the spoils from his efforts.

Across the tombolo St Ninian laid on his own little drama for us. We paused to view the remains of the 12th Century chapel, which is thought to be located over a prehistoric site. Curiously it is remembered chiefly for the ten year old boy who, while helping on an excavation in 1958, discovered a fabulous haul of Pictish treasure. The island was abandoned in 1700 when the peat ran out so it is now the preserve of sheep – and of nesting Great Skuas. I took the opportunity to stop and scan the cliffs with my binoculars while Ian ventured on to the far end of the island. As he returned he tracked away from the cliffs unwittingly close to some skuas with ground nests, which are very difficult to detect. Three of them started to attack him, swooping from all angles very close to his head. We later learnt the tactics needed to distract these awful birds but for now Ian genuinely feared he would be injured, even knocked over. He ran away from the scene of his crime. He claims that when he reached me,

I was asleep – clearly the delusion of a troubled imagination. Despite all this, to St Ninians's Isle we award the highest accolade – tranquil, beautiful, lonely and clinging improbably to the mainland by its superb tombolo.

ESHANESS

We chose the wildest of several wild days to visit Eshaness, the most north westerly part of Shetland and as close as you can be to Iceland. As trusting souls, we allowed ourselves to be misled by the tourist map to divert to Lunna House, the secret location of the Norwegian-Shetland war time resistance. We assumed, wrongly, that the isolated mansion might offer access to interested tourists. We succeeded only in amusing the baffled house owners, who hoped we were seeking B and B.

At Braewick we found an excellent coffee stop by the elevated camping site. The rain was by now horizontal, car and shop doors were taking flight and prospects for camping decidedly optimistic. The café provides a spectacular, wind proofed, southerly panorama of fields, cliffs and sea. We could make out the legendary red granite stacks known as the Drongs, dramatically lashed by white water.

The last few miles to the light house at Eshaness were boggy and bleak, with rain so fierce it was difficult even to drive. The horizon promised better however so we elegantly donned our waterproof gear and boots in the confines of the car. Soon, with the wind and sun across our backs and on springy turf, we made our way along the deeply indented cliffs towards the Villians of Ure. Conversation was rendered nearly impossible by the noise of wind and sea but we managed to convey to each other our excitement at the wild majesty of it all.

This stays in my mind as the most extreme demonstration I have seen of Atlantic power against a stubborn, jagged shoreline. White waves channelled relentlessly into narrowing rocky alcoves and through improbable arches, exploding in a riot of vertical swirling water that easily reached the fifty metre cliff tops. Stray boulders littered our route, lifted from the sea in the fiercest gales. Inland our

Dramatic stack and arch near Eshaness

Force 9 storm along coast at Eshaness

eyes were drawn across the well-drained moors to a substantial working farm – a supremely lonely and courageous enterprise. We took time to feel the force of this violent environment but turned back to reach the lighthouse just as the next mountain of black cloud swallowed the scene.

Reluctantly we drove away, still relishing our brief contact with these elemental forces of nature, on the very edge of the UK. After a mile or so we turned aside to the comparatively sheltered little bay at Stenness. Two upturned fishing boats in good order, stood alongside an abandoned shoreside stone house in the lee of which a few brave sheep nestled. Somehow the scene captured the spirit of Shetland's past – an isolated tiny settlement perched at sea level. Fishermen first; farmers second. The modern croft was secured in a small nook thirty metres above the beach, a good place to hide out on a day of these extremes.

Roofless cottage and boats: symbolic of traditional Shetland way of life, fishing first, farming second

SULLOM VOE

Sullom Voe is a huge and exceptionally well-sheltered inlet with access only from the north. The industrial complex of the oil terminal, though incongruous in the midst of such emptiness, does not overwhelm its vast landscape. The docking stations for the tankers stretch out into the Voe and the pilot tugs, large craft in their own right, line up ready to receive the next of the giants. Above the on-shore storage tanks stand two sinister chimneys perpetually burning off gases released in the processing of the oil. So on this bleak, distant installation has rested the wealth and well-being of the UK for a generation. The throughput of oil and gas has already peaked of course and we are well into consuming the second half of this irreplaceable bounty.

Shetland has rightly taken its slice of the revenues from the oil of the northern seas and has invested much into its own infrastructure, while retaining a substantial amount for its future needs. We noted just one curious anomaly. The price of fuel at the pumps here is about fifteen per cent higher than in England. We speculated how far the oil travels before it is returned for the use of the islanders – perhaps even to Rotterdam?

Sullom Voe has another claim to fame. In the Second World War it was the base from which the Catalina and Sunderland Flying Boats were launched to hunt down German u-boats and carry out missions into occupied Norway. Losses of planes and crew were high but the contribution to the war effort was hugely significant. A sombre, weather-torn roadside memorial provides a modest tribute to RAF Coastal Command.

PAPA STOUR

We made an early start to catch the ferry from Burrafirth, a secluded little harbour, to Papa Stour, a small island on the rim of West Mainland. Once again we performed some minor contortions in the car to kit ourselves in full waterproofs. The ferry carried just four vehicles, necessarily chained to the decks, and a few foot passengers. It is a heavy duty, powerful boat, not unlike a military landing craft and it made light work of the eight kilometre crossing. The mist and rain did not augur well but we were well prepared and Jeeves had of course produced an ample packed lunch.

The only surprise when we landed was the visitor rest-room, a cabin fitted with a sink, chairs and information, to protect folk such as us from the worst of the elements – a welcome innovation. The eastern zone of the island comprises a few dwellings and a surfeit of lush pasture, well drained and fenced. It is separated from the untended part of the island by a hill dyke. To the west – our intended destination – the land rose steadily through rough moorland into the low clouds. We took the only available track westward for about two kilometres. Then, before it had steered us over the last walls and fences, it just shrugged and left us to our own devices. Ian is in his element in such shapeless country and we held a good line above a myriad of little lochans towards the highest cliffs in the west. My role was to carry the rucsac and follow on, although I monitored his navigation closely. That's real leadership.

Ian is, as careful readers will recall, less at ease with Great Skuas. So carving a route across one of their primary breeding grounds in Shetland was brave. At one point I could see upwards of a dozen birds aloft within thirty metres of us. This time we each held a trekking pole aloft, like an umbrella, which deterred them from swooping. If only gannets could learn such tactics.

Our reward on the west coast of Papa Stour was cliff scenery distinctive, possibly unique, in the UK. Here be sea caves, multiple arches, steepling sea stacks and probably monsters as well. The map marks 'subterranean passages' (which we could not really see from the land) and several 'geos' – huge holes eroded inland from the cliffs, through which the sea surges in the wildest conditions. We were a day late to see a geo in full action but they are impressive. The largest here is about eighty metres long and twenty five across. The weather had lifted by the time we approached this great cavity; it would be an interesting feature to encounter in thick mist.

We paused for a drink in the shelter of a ruin at Hamna Voe. This was the site of a successful 19th Century fish curing station. It has a gently shelving red stony beach ideal for drying the salted fish, which were then transported by sail to the Scottish mainland. The scale of the enterprise became obvious as we picked out more and more ruined outbuildings, as well as the main house above the shore. At a first view this seemed just another lonely inlet. In half an hour we had cloaked it with visions of a substantial industry and population.

Today a lonely figure was gathering debris from the bay and bagging it ready for collection by boat. (There is no track out here). Hamna Voe looks to be the place where most of the marine rubbish from the north west Atlantic ends up. Fishing nets cut from trawlers accumulate a lot of mundane plastic junk and are swept on to many west facing beaches. But Hamna Voe must be the unhappy prize winner in these parts. We chatted to the beachcomber, who works for the island's Amenity Trust, about his Herculean labour. He waved an arm towards the old croft where he stays for the week. We saw no building with a roof but presume one exists. Given the scale of the task and the remoteness of the bay it is surprising that he has to spend the whole week alone. He was the only person we saw all day, and probably we were his only contacts.

We edged our way back by stages to the little harbour and the visitor hut. By now the sun was quite strong. I hovered above the jetty in case otters should appear. According to the guide book they often frolic on the quay here and even board the boats to negotiate for fish. Such cheerful hallucinations do not convince me but it is always worth a try. The return journey on the ferry brought glorious and surprising views of various shorelines that had been hidden in the morning mist. Burrafirth harbour, we now realised, lies at the end of a labyrinth of protective rocky shoulders.

A very satisfying little adventure.

BEGINNINGS AND ENDINGS

Now came Ian's turn to re-visit a name from the past. Glynne, the friend and colleague with whom Ian and Jane had shared Oxford and five years in the Solomon Islands, now lives in Shetland. They had lost contact with each other for most of four decades but in the last few years had occasionally met again. So we now headed for a village very much at the end of the line and to a house at the very limits of the settlement. Just a stone's throw from a beautiful and sheltered bay. Next stop Iceland.

The visit was particular poignant because Glynne's wife Judith was in the final stages of a ten year battle with leukaemia. Her son settled in Shetland a few years ago so Judith determined to share as fully as possible in the lives of her grandchildren by moving here. Though painfully frail, she greeted us with much warmth and delight and then retreated to rest with the aid of morphine. I sensed even in those few moments that this was a strong and lovely person.

In such an emotionally charged situation it was inevitable that the conversation – mainly between Ian and Glynne of course – would rebound from reminiscences of the Solomons to life in Shetland and to despairing hopes for Judith. They sampled some old whiskies to dull the feelings and we shared a marvellous fish pie made by our host to a secret recipe.

Glynne is Irish by origin but spent much of his life based in the USA and travelling to work assignments all round the globe, a habit and enthusiasm he still retains. He and Ian are proud of their efforts in the Solomons. Glynne said repeatedly that he would love to go back just one more time to see how much had survived. 'Did we waste our time or is there just something left of what we tried to create?' He is genuinely angry at the rapid and ill-planned granting of independence before systems of policing, justice and self governance were consolidated. Had we been allowed more time could we have avoided some of the corruption and abuses of power that later prevailed? Glynne, from first hand experience, is also scathing about most of the NGOs which lack the knowledge and skills to put aid where it will be effective. Ian would love to join him on a return venture.

The locals welcomed Glynne and Judith to their community and they have clearly made great efforts to build good relationships. Glynne rehearsed some frustrations over the planning laws that require him to conserve his house and outbuilding to the highest vernacular standards, while the adjoining premises, used as a store not a dwelling, are falling to rack and ruin. Shetland, above all, is no place to neglect your roof. He is not convinced that the best use is being made by Shetland of the oil bonus; in particular the culture of subsidies for crofting disguise the underlying issues about how to sustain agriculture here in the longer term.

As the light began to fade and the day chilled the remoteness and solitude of these islands took hold on my senses. This wild beauty, adrift between Scotland and Norway, looking to the Arctic and ever open to the elements, is not a comfortable place for all its inspirational character. It is profoundly different from anywhere else in the UK, even the other clusters of Scottish islands.

Judith was due for a further blood transfusion the following week. This involves a 50 kilometre road journey to Sumburgh, a ninety minute flight to Edinburgh, where they have a flat, and then transfer to the hospital. And of course the return. My heart sank as I thought how tough this would be for her. It would be wonderful if her condition could be rescued at least for a time; but I could not help wishing for her to find her peace here overlooking the beach, the sea and the small quay where, at dawn, otters really do frolic.

The farewells were distressing for Ian, and for Glynne. We stole off quietly into a sombre, rainy evening taking our own measure of that long journey from north to south Shetland.

(Judith lived for a further ten months).

FRAGMENTS AND REFLECTIONS

Our final full day dawned wet, with low dark cloud cover – the sort of day we had feared might afflict our whole week. Happily this gloomy start was by stages transformed so that we enjoyed bright sunshine in the afternoon. We decided against a long trip to the northernmost islands in favour of a day connecting with places and features we had so far by-passed.

The start was Scalloway, the ancient capital, which we had seen only fleetingly in the foulest weather. Its harbour and lofty castle make a haunting silhouette against the evening sun and the sea. The castle dates from 1600, built by the notoriously cruel Patrick Stewart, Earl of Orkney and Lord of Shetland, using forced labour. Legend has it that the mortar was mixed with blood and eggs. We greeted the two tourists from the Noss boat and Sumburgh Head as old friends. They had collected the castle key from the local inn. Only the central fort remains; the original outer defences incorporate the quay. A few 18th Century dwellings, built for local lairds, and the fish merchant's 19th Century cottages give the little town some character but it has been left behind by bustling Lerwick.

In the north of Ireland I had failed Helmut in his pursuit of a fish and chip lunch. Ian is made of sterner stuff and, on advice from sources close to the Lerwick Tourist Office, we chose one of the three fish shops and sat outside in the sun enjoying some very fresh, very large and quite exceptional haddock in the crispiest batter. Sorry Helmut, this was the best. I think it may be Ian's most abiding memory of Lerwick and could yet lure him back again.

We returned to a more elevated plane once more by exploring the extraordinary stone constructions on the promontory in the Loch of Clickimin on the edge of Lerwick. The original Bronze Age farmhouse dates from at least 700BC. It was superseded by an Iron Age ring fort or broch, much of which remains in place. The site was surrounded by water until the 19th Century when the level was dropped to create the causeway. The rings of the broch are immensely solid and enduring. The whole place is very evocative despite its rather suburban backdrop.

Time did not permit a trip to the famed isle of Mousa, on which stands the best preserved broch in the UK. The island is also the nocturnal roost of huge numbers of storm petrels. Instead we headed for the No Ness peninsula that looks across to Mousa. The area is uncharacteristically crowded with tiny lanes and small settlements, presumably because of its two south facing harbours. The cliffs at No Ness are glorious – gnarled, broken and fragile but offering wonderful views into sharp gullies and, far in the north, to the unmistakable outline of bird city at Noss. The nest sites here are more generously spaced but quite precarious. Fulmars are the dominant group in residence, struggling as ever to make a convincing landing near their nests. Gannet and shag dived off shore. We registered that we had started to take this rich avian entertainment for granted.

By now Shetland was starting to feel familiar. The open treeless landscapes, hundreds of tiny seashore settlements each with its own small pier, and the sparse population (outside Lerwick) shaped the sense of difference for us. The sea is always close but it is not just one sea. The awesome power of a strong westerly storm is only moments away from the calm shelter of the southerly coves and the shadow of the easterly cliffs. Even then you pass many inland waters offering a slightly gentler life for ducks and waders. Venture further east, as at Noss, and you suddenly are struck by the full force of the Norwegian Sea. There are no easy journeys out from Shetland. The skills of seamanship, learnt over generations, are immeasurable to we mere intruders from the UK mainland.

We reflected quite often that we might well have been in Norway. The tantalisingly long summer days, with barely four hours of muted darkness, the refined housing and high quality infrastructure all serve to confuse. This is not the Scotland we know well. We celebrated the long evenings and the beautiful light of the early mornings, but few people can make use of twenty hours of daylight. Inevitably we contemplated the converse of this. What must life be like in those deep dark days of winter? Our sense of equilibrium could not really cope with these important differences. How long would it take to adjust?

The place names in Shetland are a delightful and extravagant brew. The mixture of Norse, English and remnants of Pictish with other lost

Mare and foal; sturdiest of all Shetlanders

local tongues is intriguing – definitely an award winner. Imagine a short stroll or a sail from Kettla Ness past Tinklee Geo to The Heugg, then on to Fugla Stack, passing Clettnadel to Womni, ending at Lotra of Minn – an example chosen at random from the O.S. map.

We enjoyed the quiet good nature of the Shetlanders we met. They are not (in late May at least) so inundated with tourists as to have developed that artificial protective veneer of more populous holiday communities. A strong sense of confident identity comes across as welcoming. I think they are still able to appreciate people coming to enjoy their unique environment, even when they do ask awkward questions.

Early on in our stay it struck me that the landscapes across much of Mainland are very similar – engaging to the eye, shapely, very green, sparsely populated and almost always edged by the sea. We discovered some variety as we travelled north but the real contrasts are delivered by the ever changing weather. If you sit for a typical hour observing the same scene the light, the colours, the natural focus, the sense of space all shift magically. If the clouds drop and stay, the clever tactic is to make the short journey to the opposite coast where the mood will probably be different.

We treated ourselves to a last evening meander across the curved bay and the headland of the terns where we had started the week. Ian even took to the water, though only up to his knees. My ring rusty life saving skills would not be called upon. The angle of the light now picked out the array of ruined dwellings scattered over the slope above the bay; and as we turned around we saw again a whole cluster – a hamlet – of roofless stone cottages, one or two of which are being restored. When these many remote, now abandoned, settlements were alive Shetland must have been so different – local self-sufficiency at sea and on land, a daily battle to sustain the basics of life, intermittent travel by sea to Lerwick or Scalloway to trade surpluses and stock up essentials, but little awareness of the worlds beyond – even Orkney would be foreign territory. There were no major clearances or famines here so the great changes from isolation to community, from barter to a money economy, must have been incremental.

In warm sunshine we sat and watched the sea, in relatively gentle mood, sweep across some rocks. Close by two oyster catcher, uncharacteristically still and quiet, watched it all too, gathering strength for their next noisy panic. Birds must take some of their rest in the twenty hours of daylight presumably. The dawn chorus at 3.15am sounds vigorous and compulsory – can they really be so cheerful after four hours sleep?

We woke on the final morning not so long after the birds and drove south in wonderful early light and on totally empty roads for our flight. Sumburgh is a very civilised and comfortable airport, presumably another bonus from the oil. We acknowledged some apprehension at the prospect of returning to our own normalities. The pace of life here is definitely calm, despite the weather, and we had settled into a slower, uncrowded, traffic-free rhythm. Everything still answers to the elemental forces, especially the winds, in Shetland; elsewhere we can often pretend otherwise.

Edinburgh came as a shock, despite our rehearsed anticipation of the change of pace. The airport was heaving and we battled across the dense, confused streams of human traffic to the exit. At once we confronted our first traffic jam for seven days, headed by dozens of taxis with every variety of bus and coach, horns sounding, low gear exhausts swilling in the air, tempers fraying. If this is civilisation, speed me back to Shetland. A place to treasure – but it was so good to see trees again.

11. SURPRISES AND CONNECTIONS

I took myself back to that view from the youth hostel in Capel Curig to reflect on how far and how well I had travelled on this venture. The rain was still swirling across the towering forested slopes of Moel Siabod – always a special place for me. The best journeys are well planned but always open to the unexpected, to improvisation. In that lies their richness – being taken by surprise and seeing the familiar in a new light.

Three years ago, just into retirement, I mapped out this little adventure with a genuine sense of excitement for both the destinations and the chance to spend time with important friends. The notion of writing a book was just a pipe dream. Digital photography was a mountain still to be climbed. The responses of my fellow travellers encouraged me. Some fell by the wayside because of work and family commitments. Aileen does not feel the call of the high seas and wild islands, especially those of the wet Scottish variety, and was happy to wave me off. She was however envious of the other Irish journeys. I always enjoy plundering the maps and guidebooks and working on the logistics of travel, so this web of plans in itself became a new hobby.

In three years much can change. Our discussions around the theme of the 'most favoured generation' took us, as I hoped, in a hundred different directions; but over these last months the consensus about the threat of climate change has overtaken other considerations. The writing has been on the wall since the 1970s. Now it is almost too late – so we have our most urgent challenge still to face. The party really is over. The other acerbic, but hardly unfair, observation about the favoured generation is that it has also been the grumpiest and most difficult to please. But not the people I travelled with.

So looking across the venture what took me most by surprise?

The greatest visual revelations came from the islands beyond the Scottish mainland. They share an elemental beauty heightened by the constant intrusion of the seas on all sides. The skies stretch forever. Orkney is distinctively lush and Shetland somehow more Scandinavian than Scottish. The tombolo linking St Ninian's Isle is fabulous. The western isles comprise many contrasts. The west has more rewarding land despite the scouring Atlantic storms; the east is gnarled and thin soiled. The southern islands scarcely peer above the menacing seas, then mountainous Harris with its amazing beaches; and peat laden Lewis. The loudest gasp came when disbelieving, we spotted the cliffs of St Kilda out in the deep Atlantic.

Watching wildlife always offers surprises. I grew from innocence to familiarity with the truly villainous Great Skuas over these journeys. We were gifted the shock of seeing a sociable corncrake on North Uist. The otters on the Tweed below the Union Bridge provided a mesmerising spectacle, equalled by the sparkling ribbon of shearwater heading for their roosts in the half light along Ramsay Sound. The swannery at Abbotsbury may not seem very wild but it is special because the birds have gathered there for millennia. So often the best moments on these journeys were those very slow sessions meandering along a remote beach or cliffs. Nothing is happening until you stay still; then your eyes open to a whole circus of activity.

The most memorable features from Ireland have to include that first view of the Burren, a vast limestone dome made beautiful by the changing light, the turbulent seas and the green shoots of spring. I was surprised by the picturesque Boyne valley, site of an extensive Neolithic community, but also of the much replayed battle of 1690. Only when I saw the landscapes of the Wicklow Hills did their troubled histories come to life. Again my perceptions about the struggle of the Bogside community to achieve parity within Derry shifted when I saw its location below the towering walls of the city stronghold.

To be able to read a landscape or community fully you have either to spend your life in it – as Evan Roberts did – or learn from those who have. So I have been moved by the extraordinary stories of ordinary people who have risen to the challenges of their chance positions in place and time. I frequently rehearsed the idea on these journeys that my parents' generation was singularly heroic in wartime. These journeys though have revealed such heroism and accomplishment recurs across the millennia here. The great literatures of Greece and Rome dominate our awareness of ancient history but the less celebrated lives of our own Neolithic ancestors are every bit as complex and fascinating. There are just fewer clues to help understand them.

It was Skara Brae which opened my eyes to the possibility that I could come closer to understanding our Neolithic predecessors. These were no cryptic clues or enigmatic stone monuments; rather the intimate, preserved detail of everyday life around 3000BC. Visiting more of their homelands – isolated communities separated by vast distances – revealed much stronger similarities than I expected. Only a substantial flow of ideas between tribal groupings can explain their signal, shared, achievements – the stone circles and chambers. These tell of a sophisticated knowledge of astronomy, the governing force in the later Neolithic world. So the enigma starts to yield to research and to science. The scale of Neolithic settlement was much more prolific than I realised. These people were not camping out; they were shaping the landscape. Was there even, occasionally, a favoured Neolithic generation benefiting from the exhaustive labours of their ancestors?

The recent TV series by Ray Mears ('Wild Food') set out to compare the survival skills of 20th Century low technology societies alongside evidence from stone-age archaeology. The extraordinary connections lead on to speculation about how these peoples communicated. There is no evidence of written language; but the memorised oral traditions of the aborigines in Australia are extensive and elaborate. Maybe our Neolithic settlers here had chants for journeys, for rituals, for agriculture.

Later, the Celts still relied in large part on oral communication not just for the practicalities of life but for sharing their histories and creativity. I will risk stretching this line about memorised learning even further. In 1746 as the opposing armies assembled at Culloden they exchanged abusive taunts across the moor. Then some of the Highland clansmen started to chant their genealogy, back through several centuries. They believed that courage flowed down through the generations and would be invoked by recalling the names. We today regard writing as a key element of social cohesion; but spoken language, given its full scope, probably served the Ancients well.

Today's people took us by surprise as well. We enjoyed so many interesting encounters and warm welcomes. Those confident young students on Inisheer could talk happily with two old passers-by. There were islanders who declared a stronger allegiance to Europe than to Scotland or Britain. The people of Berwick still struggle with an identity torn between England and Scotland. I picture that ninety seven year old man determined to see out his days in his lifelong home overlooking the wild Griminish rocks on Uist. A pity we did not stay to listen longer to him. We were alert for evidence of residual hostility to the English as the former occupiers. Declan readily opened the door to the Bogside for us. I know, nonetheless, that hostility to we English can be found in urban Scotland and Ireland; and maybe the fish vendor in Tarbert still has a point to make.

We chose to go to the edges of Britain so it was certain we would experience the diversity in the ways people live their lives and view the world. The surprise here is that such places identify at all with Edinburgh or London or the wider world. The pace and purpose of life look very different. They must listen to the news, or to parliament, or to the weather forecasts in amazement, wondering if their communities have anything at all in common with remote urban Britain.

Was I surprised by the story of John Rae, the Orcadian Arctic explorer denied his due place in history by the crushing weight of the Victorian Establishment? For me it came to symbolise the weary omniscience of the London power-brokers, who could also rationalise so cleverly the Famine, the Clearances, even Slavery. Now we tend to make grave apology for such historical misdeeds. But Sir Humphrey still rules. Radical challenges, especially from outsiders, still produce defensive disdain from the Establishment: Widgery on Bloody Sunday, Hutton on the case for war in Iraq, the de Menezes enquiry, real electoral reform, the real implications of climate change. Plus ça change.

Finally, surprises also surfaced in conversations with my fellow travellers. I knew that there were gaps to fill in their stories but I did not realise how inadequately I had listened in the past. It was satisfying to join more of the pieces together and to learn about the turning points. It was also very re-affirming, more than I could have hoped, to sense their enjoyment of our exploration at the fringes of these wonderful islands.

THE BEST OF THE BEST?

I hope if you have come this far with me you may have resolved that those oft postponed, home-based journeys to places long held in your imagination must soon become a reality. So I will risk some advice at the end of my venture:

To attune to the Ancients go first to Orkney.

If you are drawn to communities in recovery listen first hand to the people of the Bogside.

For vast colonies of sea-birds in the most spectacular location go to Noss, from Lerwick.

To understand more about how famine is allowed to happen amid plenty, go to Clare (or any part of western Ireland).

To glimpse shearwater returning en masse to roost at dusk, go on to Ramsay Sound in bad weather.

To experience an authentic youth hostel in a perfect location, go to Rhenigidal, on Harris.

If you just enjoy the journeys, take the ferry from Tarbert to Skye.

If, like me, you have still to make it to St Kilda, go soon (but slowly).

And take an old friend or two with you.

Whatever, wherever, search for some roots and shape some dreams.

SOURCES USED

Journeys, photographs, conversations, observations, sites.
Ordnance Survey maps.
Rough Guides – Scotland, Ireland, Great Britain.
Site guides – eg National Trust, English Heritage, CADW, Historic
Scotland, independent, archaeological.
Interpretative exhibitions, museums, reconstructions, websites.
Wildlife and Field Guides.

OTHER TEXTS

Atlas of Prehistoric Britain: John Manley (Phaidon)
Fatal Passage: Ken McCoogan(Bantam)
The Irish Famine: Peter Gray (Thames and Hudson)
The Scottish Islands: H. Haswell-Smith (Canongate)
Lighthouse Stevensons: Bella Bathurst (Harper Collins)
The Emergency: Ireland 1939-45 Brian Girvin (Pan)
Northern Ireland 1968-99 Bew and Gillespie (Gill/Macmillan)
The Sea Kingdoms – History of Celtic Britain and Ireland: Alistair
Moffat (Harper Collins)
Wild Food: Ray Mears 2007 (Hodder and Stoughton)